D0691366

DEEP FRIED INDULGENCES

Christie Katona
Thomas Katona

BRISTOL PUBLISHING ENTERPRISES
San Leandro, California

A Nitty Gritty® Cookbook

Printed in the United States of America.

ISBN 1-55867-116-1

Cover design: Frank Paredes
Cover photography: John Benson
Food stylist: Suzanne Carreiro
Illustrator: James Balkovek

CONTENTS

AN INTRODUCTION TO DEEP FRYING

Hot, juicy, golden, crisp, succulent and satisfying — these are the words that describe the appeal of deep fried foods and the reason why America consumes so much of them — from French fries, onion rings and chicken to calamari, tempura and fried won tons.

We have compiled a wide selection of recipes covering breakfast treats, snacks and appetizers, entrées, international specialties, side dishes, vegetables and desserts.

If you are concerned about watching your fat and calorie intake, take heart; by preparing the food yourself and following a few cooking guidelines, you can control both the type of oil used and the amount of oil absorption in the food. Remember, you have the ultimate control over the foods used for deep frying, as well as how much and how often you eat. It is also easier to get exactly what you want when you prepare it yourself.

By judiciously selecting healthful foods as the focus of your daily diet, and by limiting your portions of foods with a high fat and caloric content, you can occasionally enjoy *Deep Fried Indulgences!*

SELECTING A DEEP FRYER

The basic distinction between deep fryers is the amount of added features and the capacity.

Each model has advantages. While the least expensive models lack user controls, they are very compact, easy to clean and easy to store. Other brands are insulated and have more controls and features, but some are considerably bulkier. Most manufacturers have a range of models from which to choose. Some features — for example, a nonstick surface — may be offered by the same manufacturer on another model.

Following are some general features useful in a deep fryer and some of the nice-to-have extras.

USEFUL FEATURES

adjustable temperature control
nonstick coating, on both inside and outside surface
oil level mark
seamless fryer interior (no crevices)

NICE-TO-HAVE EXTRAS

built-in timer
condensation trap
deep fry basket
locking lid
odor filter
viewing window

FEATURES THAT REQUIRE SPECIAL MENTION

At least one deep fryer model has an **angled rotating basket** that rotates the food in and out of the oil, which the manufacturer claims causes less oil absorption. The basket handle is external and folds down to be even with the front of the unit. When the handle is folded down, the basket is lowered into the oil and starts the motor, which rotates the basket. When the handle is lifted up, the basket is raised out of the oil and the whole basket and handle can be lifted out of the fryer as one assembly after the lid has been opened.

Other deep fryer models also have an **external dial** that will raise and lower the basket into the oil; however, you must open the lid and insert the basket handle to remove the basket. This type of deep fryer appears to have the best designed **odor filter**. The activated charcoal filter canister has an indicator that changes color when the filter needs to be replaced. The canister is easily replaced from the top of the lid without resorting to tools, which is not true on some of the other available models.

Some deep fryers have a **seamless fryer interior**, which is useful when cleaning. Other fryers have crevices around the fryer bowl that, when cleaned, appear to be completely devoid of food particles. However, when oil is added and heated, food particles come bubbling out of the crevices and have to be skimmed off.

Some deep fryers have a **locking lid**, but also allow you to remove the lid if you choose to fry with it open.

A **viewing window** is somewhat useful to view cooking progress while avoiding exposure to spattering oil. Most insulated units have viewing windows; however, the viewing windows can become clouded with water vapor when cooking foods with a high water content, making them almost useless until most of the water has been cooked out of the food. One of the manufacturers recommends coating the inside of the window with cooking oil. This gives only marginal improvement. Still, the windows are useful on occasion.

Visit local shops and discount stores and take a close look at a number of models, keeping in mind those items mentioned above.

COOKING OILS AND COOKING TEMPERATURES

The difference between stovetop frying and deep frying is that with deep frying the food is totally immersed in and surrounded by hot oil. For this reason, deep frying is fast because the heated oil is very efficient at transferring its stored heat to the food and because all, or a large part, of the food's surface area is in contact with the hot oil at the same time. If done properly, deep frying quickly seals the outside of the food, which seals the oil out and the moisture in. As a result, the food is literally cooked in its own steam. Both the oil and the temperature used for deep frying affect the quality of the fried food.

There is a wide variety of vegetable oil and shortening at the supermarket and at specialty shops. For deep frying, we recommend a good-quality, blended vegetable oil. This type of oil is pressed, refined, bleached and even deodorized at the factory to the point that it is sometimes difficult to tell one type from another after they have been processed. In general, they all have a very bland taste. However, the smoking points of these oils vary between brands and types.

The smoking point of an oil is the point where the temperature is high enough to start breaking down the oil and is so named because a light blue haze of smoke can be seen coming off the surface of the oil at the breakdown temperature. If your cooking oil reaches this point, it is time to either reduce the temperature or change the oil. If you continue to apply heat after this point, the oil could potentially ignite and cause injury to you or your kitchen.

Basically, any good brand name vegetable oil will work for deep frying since all have been designed to remain stable within the normal deep frying temperature range (300° to 390°F). Stay away from butter, margarine and lard since these have relatively low smoking temperatures. Our recommendation for deep frying oils, in rough order of preference, is a blended vegetable oil, corn oil, peanut oil, canola (rapeseed) oil and, finally, sunflower oil. In actuality, they are all pretty close to each other. Soybean oil can also be used, but it tends to foam during deep frying, so you should probably choose another oil. Olive oil is also stable at high frying temperatures and can certainly be used, but it is strongly flavored compared to the blended vegetable oils and will impart its own flavor to the food.

The temperature of the oil also has a significant impact on the quality of the fried food. To deep fry properly, the temperature of the oil should be adjusted to match the food being cooked. If the temperature is too high, the outside of the food will seal, crisp and brown quickly, but the inside will be underdone. If the temperature is too low, the food will take longer to seal and cook and will absorb more oil due to the extended cooking time; the outcome will be greasy, soggy, heavy food.

Make sure the oil is at the correct temperature before starting to fry. Modern deep fryers usually have an indicator light that turns off when the set temperature is reached. For less expensive units, wait 10 to 15 minutes after the unit is turned on or use a deep fryer thermometer (recommended) to check the proper temperature. If your fryer does not have a thermostat, and you lack a thermometer, one trick is to place a 1-inch cube of white bread (minus crust) into the heated oil. If the cube turns a nice golden brown after 60 seconds, you're ready for deep frying.

Since there are so many variations in features and in capacity of home deep fryers, and in the food being cooked, it is possible to set only general temperature guidelines for deep frying. Following are some of the factors that can affect the oil temperature and cooking time.

- ***The quantity of oil in relation to the quantity of food fried***. Generally, the greater the ratio of oil to food, the greater the heat energy stored in the oil for transfer to the food. This means that there will be less of a drop in oil temperature when food is added, which generally translates to less greasy food.

- ***The thickness and shape of the food***. More cooking time is required to cook thick pieces of food than thin pieces.

- ***The amount of water in the food to be cooked***. The more water in the food, the more heat is required for a given quantity of food. For example, meat, fish and some vegetables contain a lot of water.

- ***The temperature of the food***. Generally, only small portions of frozen foods can be fried at one time due to the drop in oil temperature caused by the frozen food.

- ***The power capacity of the fryer***. The more power available for heating, the quicker the fryer will return to the proper temperature after food has been added. The fryers these recipes were tested on ranged from 1200 to 1650 watts in power.

NOTE: The 1650 watt units approach the current carrying capacity of most home outlets (15 amperes); therefore, using additional kitchen electrical equipment on the same circuit at the same time could trip your circuit breaker. When shopping for a deep fryer, the wattage of the unit will be stamped or labeled on the side or bottom of the unit. Look for the Underwriter's Laboratory (UL) symbol.

- **The desired amount of crust on the food**. Generally, higher deep frying temperatures provide more crust on most foods.

- **The use of breadcrumb coatings**. Breadcrumb coatings tend to increase cooking time slightly because the coating itself must be cooked, and the coating slows the heat transfer to the food it coats.

REUSING, FILTERING AND STORING OILS

Continual exposure to high heat, water and burned food particles suspended in the oil eventually cause cooking oil to break down. Some of the symptoms of oil breakdown are excessive smoking at a normal frying temperature, strong discoloration of the oil, excessive foaming around frying food, and a stale or rancid smell to the oil. When this occurs, replace with fresh oil.

Generally, you can reuse the oil a dozen or so times before having to change it completely, provided you take care to filter the oil between uses and you maintain the recommended ratio of oil to food when cooking. Each time you use the fryer, a certain amount of the oil will have to be replenished, which tends to fortify the existing oil.

Special paper filters are sold for filtering cooking oil, but you can also use a fine mesh strainer as a substitute. After using the deep fryer, wait until the oil has cooled to the point where it will not burn but is still somewhat hot.

To store the oil in the refrigerator in a separate container, place the filter paper into a strainer over the storage container and pour the oil out of the fryer through the filter and into the storage container. Cover tightly and place in the refrigerator.

We do not recommend storing oil in the fryer, due to safety concerns.

In general, cooking oils break down from exposure to heat and light or can turn rancid by exposure to air. As a result, oils should be stored in a cool place away from light in airtight containers. Olive oils are particularly susceptible to turning rancid. Our recommendation is to store olive oil in small containers and keep them in the refrigerator. Olive oil will semi-solidify in the refrigerator and turn milky-white in appearance; however, the oil will return to its natural state when brought back to room temperature.

DEEP FRYING HINTS, TECHNIQUES AND GENERAL SAFETY TIPS

Deep frying is something of an art. The best teacher is experience, but by following the cooking tips below, first time users can be successful on their first try.

- Some deep fryers come with a plastic lid to cover the fryer during storage. Be sure to remove this lid before heating the unit, and *never* use the plastic lid while frying.

- To fill the fryer, pour cooking oil or spoon shortening into the unheated deep fryer *before* you apply power by switch or plug the cord into the wall outlet. Follow the manufacturer's recommendation for the amount of oil. Most deep fryers have a line showing the optimum level, and some have both a minimum and maximum oil fill line. In the absence of a line, the general rule is to fill the fryer to at least $1/3$ full but not over $1/2$ full. This will provide enough oil to allow the food to move but not enough to cause the oil to spill over when food is added.

- If your deep fryer has a detachable cord, plug in the deep fryer side first before plugging the cord into the wall outlet. When you are done frying, detach the cord from the wall outlet first, but wait until the unit is cool to remove the cord from the fryer.

- If you have young children, do not let the deep fryer cord hang over the counter edge where kids can pull the unit off the counter. Most modern units are deliberately designed with a short cord to prevent this from happening. Don't circumvent this safety feature by using an extension cord.

- The less expensive deep fryers are not insulated and will burn you if handled anywhere but at the insulated handles. These units are also fairly hot on the bottom, so it might be wise to use something beneath the fryer to insulate it from the table or counter.

- If you have small children, use an insulated deep fryer to help reduce the chance of burns.
- Avoid moving a fryer containing hot cooking oil; wait until the oil has cooled.
- Do not heat deep fryers without oil; many of the deep fryers will overheat and can be damaged. Most models contain a temperature-sensitive fuse that will protect the heating elements, but will still require a trip to the service shop to replace the internal fuse.
- Don't allow the oil to overheat. Most modern fryers have thermostats, so this is usually not a problem. However, if the oil does reach its smoking temperature and heat is continuously applied, there is the danger of igniting the oil. If this happens, smother the flames with the lid (but not the plastic one). ***Never attempt to put out a grease fire with water.***
- Because they will melt, never use plastic- or rubber-coated utensils in the hot oil.

FOOD PREPARATION TIPS

- Food that is to be deep fried should be cut in uniform sizes to promote even cooking. If pieces are cut too thick, the inside may not be done even though the outside may look golden brown.
- Dry the surface of the food. Excess water from damp food will cause spattering of the hot oil and tends to prevent the food from becoming crisp. Foods containing large

amounts of water (meat, fish and some vegetables) should be used with a breadcrumb coating.

- If your deep fryer has a basket, place the food around the perimeter of the basket to help ensure even frying. Never overload the basket since this will lower the temperature of the oil and could cause oil spillage when the food is lowered into the oil.
- If your deep fryer does not have a basket, use a slotted metal spatula both to lower food into the fryer and to spoon it back out. Before spooning in the food, dip the utensil in the hot oil first. This will help prevent food from sticking to the utensil.
- When ready, lower the food into the oil slowly. Dropping the basket or food into the oil quickly could cause spattering or oil spillage.
- Leave enough room in the fryer so the food can move around freely. If pieces touch, they will cook unevenly. Use a suitable utensil to separate the food if this occurs.
- While cooking, remove loose particles of food or coatings with a slotted spoon or strainer. Pieces of food left in the hot oil will burn and discolor the oil, and reduce the usable life of the cooking oil.
- After the food has cooked, drain the oil from the food while the food is hot. Some deep fryers have baskets that can be raised above the oil and drained. For the less expensive units, spoon out the food onto absorbent paper towels.
- Generally, the rule is to fry in several batches instead of one or two large batches, to

prevent the oil temperature from dropping. This is especially true for frozen foods. As you prepare small batches, you can keep them warm in a low oven (200°F) on a paper towel-lined cookie sheet. After each batch, add oil as necessary and wait for the temperature to rise to the correct point for whatever food you are frying. On units with thermostats, a pilot light will go out when the correct temperature is reached. It is very important to allow the oil to come back up to the correct temperature before frying again. If you don't, the food will tend to be greasy and soggy.

- When you deep fry fish, keep that oil just for frying fish in the future. The "fishy" flavor picked up by the cooking oil will taint your other foods, but it will be just fine for frying additional fish.

DIRECTIONS FOR BREADCRUMB COATINGS

For light coatings, use white bread that has been dried out overnight or left in a warm oven until dry. Remove the crusts and crush in a plastic bag with a rolling pin, or place in a blender or food processor.

For a darker crumb coating, leave the crusts on the bread and toast it before making crumbs. Dark bread can also be used.

Be creative with the type of breadcrumbs you use: sourdough, egg bread, rye bread, etc. Any other type you might have on hand can add flavor and texture to your recipes. Keep a plastic bag of breads in the freezer and add it to the odds and ends, crusts, rolls, hamburger and hot dog buns, bagels and bread that is getting too old for sandwiches. Then use this bread to make breadcrumbs the next time you need them.

When preparing food for breadcrumb coatings, be sure it is as dry as possible. Have three shallow bowls ready, such as pie pans. In the first bowl, place flour — which may be seasoned, if desired. In the second bowl, place egg mixture. For a lighter coating, use egg whites only; this also helps cut cholesterol. Add a pinch of salt to the egg or egg whites to help break up the viscosity and make the egg mixture smoother. In the third bowl, place breadcrumbs.

OILS, FATS AND YOUR HEALTH

Whether you fry on the stovetop or in a deep fryer, there is always a percentage of fat transfer to the food; the cooking method and cooking time determine how much. Fats have suffered from a tarnished image in the last 10 to 15 years. Fat has developed a reputation for clogging arteries and contributing to coronary heart disease; however, fat is one of the essential nutrients for the human body.

What is the difference is between an oil and a fat? In terms of chemical structure, they are the same; the basic difference is that oils are liquid at room temperature while almost all fats are solid.

Fat is necessary for the absorption of fat-soluble vitamins. It is part of the makeup of individual cells; it is used by the body to produce other essential nutrients. It provides lubrication, necessary cushioning for vital internal organs, a steady slow-burning fuel for the body and insulation against cold. As a source of energy, fats produce twice the energy per unit weight than do either proteins or carbohydrates. Problems can occur when we consume too much of the wrong types of fat.

The fats we eat fall primarily into two categories: saturated fats and unsaturated fats. Unsaturated fats can be further broken down into the two subcategories of polyunsaturated fats and monounsaturated fats.

Some cooking oils are described as "partially hydrogenated." This is the result of a chemical process used by the manufacturers to add hydrogen to the oil to "saturate" it. The purpose is not to increase the amount of saturated fat, but to extend the shelf life of the product and prevent rancidity. Unfortunately, the term "partially hydrogenated" doesn't convey how much saturation has taken place. If the manufacturers add a small amount, the polyunsaturated oil may be converted to mostly monounsaturated oil. If they were to go to 100% hydrogenation, the oil would become a fat and would most likely be solid at room temperature.

THE RELATIONSHIP OF FAT TO CHOLESTEROL

The amount of saturated versus unsaturated fat consumed appears to have the greatest impact on the health of the human body. We know from medical studies that consuming large amounts of saturated fat has a direct correlation to high serum cholesterol levels in the blood which, in turn, increases our risk of heart disease.

Cholesterol is a substance produced by the human liver, and it is necessary to produce sex hormones and to produce substances needed by the body to build cell membranes. It is found in all animals, including fish, but not in plants. Medical studies have identified two kinds of serum cholesterol: low-density lipoprotein (LDL) and high-density lipoprotein (HDL) cholesterol. Of the two, HDL-cholesterol is considered the "good" cholesterol since it tends to prevent the buildup of fat in the arteries. LDL is termed the "bad" cholesterol because it tends to promote the buildup of fat in the arteries, contributing to coronary heart disease and arteriosclerosis (hardening of the arteries). Studies have linked high levels of cholesterol to gall stones and colon cancer, as well.

Recent medical studies have provided strong clues regarding the relationship of serum cholesterol levels in our blood to the types of fat we consume. Eating saturated fats tends to produce higher levels of the wrong kind of cholesterol in our blood stream, whereas eating polyunsaturated fats tends to lower overall cholesterol levels. Unfortunately, these same studies indicate that when we consume only polyunsaturated fats in lieu of saturated fats, the "good" HDL-cholesterol in the blood stream is reduced along with the "bad" LDL-cholesterol. But happily, these same studies indicate that when monounsaturated fats are substituted for saturated fats in our diet, the amount of LDL-cholesterol is reduced, but the amount of HDL-cholesterol in our blood appears to increase. Olive oil naturally contains a large amount of monounsaturated fat, and this may account for the fact that in Italy and Greece, where a large amount of olive oil is consumed, the serum cholesterol levels are very low.

Most labels on cooking oils now break down the total fat content to show you the amount of saturated, polyunsaturated and monounsaturated fat by weight (usually per tablespoon of oil). If they don't, perhaps there is something they don't want to tell you. If you wish to heed the advice of the latest medical studies, and are concerned about your health and that of your family, select a brand containing a large amount of monounsaturated fat and one that is labeled "all natural" versus "partially hydrogenated."

BREAKFAST TREATS

ORANGE PUFFS WITH CREAM CHEESE GLAZE

*In the process of making this book, we found that we really liked making donut holes for breakfast. They are fast, easy and delicious. As an alternative to **Cream Cheese Glaze**, shake puffs in a bag of powdered sugar to coat.*

2 cups flour
1/3 cup sugar
3 tsp. baking powder
1/2 tsp. salt
1 tsp. cinnamon
1/2 tsp. nutmeg
1/4 cup vegetable oil

1/2 cup milk
juice of 1 orange, about 1/4 cup
1 egg, beaten
grated zest (peel, colored portion only)
   of 1 orange
oil for deep frying
Cream Cheese Glaze, follows

In a large bowl, combine flour, sugar, baking powder, salt, cinnamon and nutmeg. In a small bowl, combine vegetable oil, milk, orange juice and egg until blended. Pour into dry ingredients and stir until moistened. Stir in orange zest and mix well. Heat oil in the deep fryer to 370°. Drop dough by rounded teaspoonfuls into hot oil. Fry in batches until golden brown, about 4 to 5 minutes. Drain on paper towels. While still warm, drizzle puffs with *Cream Cheese Glaze*.

CREAM CHEESE GLAZE

3 oz. cream cheese, room temperature
juice of 2 oranges, about ½ cup
1 cup powdered sugar
½ cup milk, or more as needed

In a small bowl, combine all ingredients until smooth. Mixture should be the consistency of heavy cream; add more milk if necessary. Makes 1 cup.

CALAS

These deep fried rice cakes are a specialty down South. Serve them sprinkled with powdered sugar and strawberry jam. For real authenticity, use Louisiana cane syrup. Cook the rice the day before you plan to serve these.

2 cups cooked rice, cold
3 eggs, beaten
1/2 cup sugar
1 tsp. cinnamon
1 tsp. nutmeg

1/2 tsp. vanilla extract
2 1/4 tsp. baking powder
1/2-1 cup flour
oil for deep frying
powdered sugar

In a large bowl, combine rice, eggs, sugar, cinnamon, nutmeg, vanilla and baking powder. Add just enough flour to hold batter together. Heat oil in the deep fryer to 365°. Drop batter by teaspoonfuls into hot oil. Fry in batches until crisp and golden, about 7 minutes. Drain on paper towels and sprinkle generously with powdered sugar.

BUTTERMILK PUFFS

This is a welcome treat for a special breakfast.

1 pkg. active dry yeast
¼ cup warm water
1 tsp. sugar
1 cup buttermilk
½ cup sugar
¼ cup butter, melted
4 cups sifted self-rising flour

1 tsp. cinnamon
½ tsp. nutmeg
2 eggs, beaten
½ cup finely chopped pecans
oil for deep frying
cinnamon sugar

Using a food processor or blender, combine yeast, warm water and 1 tsp. sugar. Allow to stand for 5 minutes or until foamy. Heat buttermilk until lukewarm. Add sugar and melted butter. Add buttermilk mixture to yeast mixture and add 2 cups flour. Process until mixture is smooth, about 3 minutes. Add remaining flour, cinnamon, nutmeg, eggs and pecans and combine thoroughly. Remove dough to a greased bowl, cover and allow to rise in a warm place until bubbly, about 1½ hours. Stir down dough. Heat oil in the deep fryer to 365°. Drop batter by small spoonfuls into hot oil. Fry in batches until deep golden brown, about 5 minutes. Drain on paper towels and roll in cinnamon sugar. Serve hot.

TIPSY PRUNES

These make a nice nibbler before brunch. Soak the wooden toothpicks in water for 30 minutes before frying. Serve on a bed of bright green parsley.

1 orange
2 tbs. bourbon
1 pkg. (12 oz.) pitted prunes
1 lb. bacon, slices cut in half
oil for deep frying

Grate zest (peel, colored portion only) from orange into a large bowl. Squeeze juice from orange into bowl. Add bourbon and prunes. Allow to stand at room temperature for 2 hours. Wrap each prune in a half slice of bacon and secure with a wooden toothpick. Heat oil in the deep fryer to 360°. Fry prunes in batches until bacon is crisp. Remove and drain on paper towels. Allow to cool slightly as these retain heat.

BLUEBERRY FRITTERS

Make these special fritters for a breakfast treat.

1 cup fresh blueberries
1 cup flour
2 tbs. sugar
1 tsp. baking powder
¼ tsp. nutmeg
¼ tsp. cinnamon

¼ tsp. salt
½ cup milk
1 egg, beaten
oil for deep frying
powdered sugar

Rinse berries and pat dry with paper towels. In a large bowl, combine flour, sugar, baking powder, nutmeg, cinnamon and salt. Stir together milk and egg; pour into dry ingredients and stir until combined. Gently fold in blueberries. Heat oil in the deep fryer to 370°. Drop batter by teaspoonfuls into hot oil. Fry in batches until golden, about 3 minutes. Drain on paper towels. Sprinkle with powdered sugar. Serve warm.

SCOTCH EGGS

These eggs are an English tradition. They are nice to serve at a hearty breakfast.

oil for deep frying
3 hard-cooked eggs
½ lb. pork sausage, room temperature
1 egg, beaten
1 cup fine breadcrumbs

Heat oil in the deep fryer to 375°. Wrap each egg completely with sausage meat. Dip into beaten egg and roll in breadcrumbs. Fry eggs for 3 to 4 minutes or until golden brown and sausage is done. Cut eggs in half to serve.

SNACKS

CORN DOGS

Your children will enjoy making this all-time favorite at home. Popsicle sticks are available at hobby and craft stores. Serve with ketchup, mustard and plenty of napkins. These are also fun to make using tiny cocktail franks.

1 cup flour
1 cup cornmeal
1 tbs. sugar
1 tbs. baking powder
1 tsp. salt
1 tsp. chili powder

2 eggs, beaten
1 cup milk
¼ cup vegetable oil
oil for deep frying
1 lb. hot dogs

In a large bowl, combine flour, cornmeal, sugar, baking powder, salt and chili powder. In a small bowl, beat eggs with milk and ¼ cup oil. Pour liquid ingredients into dry ingredients and whisk together until batter is smooth. Heat oil in the deep fryer to 360°. Insert a popsicle stick into each hot dog. Using the stick as a handle, dip each hot dog into batter and turn to coat evenly. Fry corn dogs several at a time until golden, about 3 to 5 minutes. Drain on paper towels.

MEXICAN WON TONS

Serve these delicious appetizers with guacamole or salsa for dipping. It's a bit time-consuming to make these, but they can be made ahead, covered with plastic wrap and refrigerated for up to two days. Or deep fry, cover, refrigerate for up to two days and reheat on a cookie sheet in a 450° oven for 5 minutes.

1 lb. pepper Jack cheese, shredded
1 pkg. (1 lb.) won ton wrappers
oil for deep frying

Place 1 tsp. cheese in the center of each won ton wrapper. Fold edge over cheese and roll to within 1 inch of the corner. Moisten edges of won ton wrapper with water and fold side corners over, overlapping the points slightly. Pinch together to seal. Place filled won tons on a cookie sheet in a single layer. To deep fry, heat oil in the deep fryer to 350°. Fry won tons in batches until crisp and golden, about 2 minutes. Drain on paper towels. Serve warm.

WON TONS ITALIAN-STYLE

Try dipping these in marinara sauce.

½ lb. fontina cheese
¼ lb. Italian salami
½ cup sun-dried tomatoes
2 cloves garlic, minced

1 pkg. (1 lb.) won ton wrappers
oil for deep frying
grated Parmesan cheese, optional

Shred cheese and place in a medium bowl. Coarsely chop salami and sun-dried tomatoes and add to cheese. Stir in minced garlic and mix well. Place 1 tsp. cheese mixture in the center of each won ton wrapper. Fold edge over cheese and roll to within 1 inch of the corner. Moisten edges of won ton wrapper with water and fold side corners over, overlapping the points slightly. Pinch together to seal. (See diagram on page 27.) Place filled won tons on a cookie sheet in a single layer. Cover with plastic wrap and refrigerate for 1 hour or up to 2 days. To deep fry, heat oil in the deep fryer to 350°. Fry won tons in batches until crisp and golden, about 2 minutes. Drain on paper towels. Serve warm. Sprinkle with Parmesan cheese, if desired.

CREAM CHEESE AND BACON WON TONS

Throw caution and calories to the wind and enjoy these delightfully different appetizers. Serve melted red or green pepper jelly as an accompaniment. Any leftover won ton wrappers may be wrapped tightly and frozen for future use.

1 lb. bacon, cooked crisp and crumbled
8 oz. cream cheese, room temperature
2 tbs. minced crystallized ginger
2 green onions, finely chopped
1 tsp. curry powder
1 pkg. (1 lb.) won ton wrappers
oil for deep frying

In a medium bowl, combine bacon, cream cheese, ginger, green onions and curry powder. Place 1 tsp. cheese mixture in the center of each won ton wrapper. Fold edge over cheese and roll to within 1 inch of the corner. Moisten edges of won ton wrapper with water and fold side corners over, overlapping the points slightly. Pinch together to seal. (See diagram on page 27.) Place filled won tons on a cookie sheet in a single layer. At this point, these may be covered with plastic wrap and refrigerated for up to 2 days. To deep fry, heat oil in the deep fryer to 350°. Fry won tons in batches until crisp and golden, about 2 minutes. Drain on paper towels. These retain heat for a long time, so allow them to cool for at least 5 minutes before serving.

GOAT CHEESE AND ROASTED
RED PEPPER WON TONS

Combine sour cream with pesto for dipping these won tons. When filling won tons with soft cream cheese fillings, chill them for at least an hour before frying.

8 oz. herb cream cheese, such as
   Rondele or Boursin
8 oz. goat cheese
2 cloves garlic, minced

$\frac{1}{4}$ cup diced roasted red pepper
1 pkg. (1 lb.) won ton wrappers
oil for deep frying

In a small bowl, combine herb cream cheese, goat cheese, garlic and red pepper. Mixture should be chunky. Place 1 tsp. cheese mixture in the center of each won ton wrapper. Fold edge over cheese and roll to within 1 inch of the corner. Moisten edges of won ton wrapper with water and fold side corners over, overlapping the points slightly. Pinch edges together to seal. (See diagram on page 27.) Place filled won tons on a cookie sheet in a single layer, cover with plastic wrap and chill for 1 hour or up to 2 days. To deep fry, heat oil in the deep fryer to 350°. Fry won tons in batches until crisp and golden, about 2 minutes. Drain on paper towels. These retain heat for a long time, so allow them to cool for at least 5 minutes before serving.

CRAB RANGOON WON TONS

*This recipe originated years ago at Trader Vic's restaurant. Carefully pick over crabmeat for any pieces of shell. Serve with **Plum Sauce**, page 100, for dipping.*

½ lb. fresh crabmeat
8 oz. cream cheese, room temperature
2 green onions, chopped
½ tsp. horseradish

½ tsp. lemon juice
⅛ tsp. hot pepper sauce
1 pkg. (1 lb.) won ton wrappers
oil for deep frying

In a small bowl, combine crabmeat, cream cheese, onions, horseradish, lemon juice and hot pepper sauce, mixing well. Mixture should still be chunky. Place 1 tsp. cheese mixture in the center of each won ton wrapper. Fold edge over cheese and roll to within 1 inch of the corner. Moisten edges of won ton wrapper with water and fold side corners over, overlapping the points slightly. Pinch edges together to seal. (See diagram on page 27.) Place filled won tons on a cookie sheet in a single layer, cover with plastic wrap and chill for 1 hour or up to 2 days. To deep fry, heat oil in the deep fryer to 350°. Fry won tons in batches until crisp and golden, about 2 minutes. Drain on paper towels. These retain heat for a long time, so allow them to cool for at least 5 minutes before serving.

WON TON CRISPS

Won ton wrappers are usually sold in the produce department or Oriental food section of the grocery store. Available in 1-pound packages, they usually contain 70 to 100 wrappers. Uncooked wrappers can be kept in the freezer; be sure to wrap them well. Here are three different ways to flavor these crispy snacks. Experiment and invent your own recipes. Serve with dips, toss in salads or grab a handful for a quick snack. Store in an airtight container. These keep well for about 3 days.

oil for deep frying
24 won ton wrappers, cut in half diagonally

1 tbs. sesame oil
2 tbs. soy sauce
2 tbs. toasted sesame seeds

VARIATION: CURRY CRISPS

¼ cup butter, melted
2 tbs. curry powder

VARIATION: ITALIAN CRISPS

¼ cup olive oil
1 clove garlic, minced
3 tbs. grated Parmesan cheese

Heat oil in the deep fryer to 375°. Quickly fry won ton wrappers in batches, stirring to keep pieces separate. When crisps are golden, about 1 minute, remove with a slotted spoon and drain on paper towels. Drizzle with oil or butter and sprinkle with seasoning. Serve warm or at room temperature.

OIL PASTRY

This dough is crispy with a slightly chewy, bread-like texture. It is ideal for making fried calzones, empanadas, meat pies, pastries or the Southern favorite, fried pies. We have included several recipes for ideas and preparations. Count on making about 30 small turnovers. Be sure to use bread flour, which contains more gluten; it is readily available at grocery stores. Do not use this recipe for baking; it is for frying only.

2 cups all-purpose flour
1 cup bread flour
1½ tsp. salt
1 oz. lard or solid shortening

3 tbs. olive oil
1 cup water
filling, as desired

In a food processor or blender, combine flours and salt. In a microwave or in a small saucepan, melt lard or shortening with olive oil; add with water to food processor or blender, and process. When dough begins to form a mass, remove to a lightly floured piece of waxed paper. Shape into a flat disk, wrap tightly in plastic wrap and allow dough to rest for 1 hour at room temperature or for up to 3 days in the refrigerator.

To use dough, lightly flour a rolling pin and your work surface. Roll dough out to

⅛-inch thickness. Cut out 3-inch circles. Reroll scraps, taking care not to stretch dough.

To fill, place a rounded spoonful of filling in the center of each circle. Moisten edges with water and fold over to form a crescent. Press firmly to seal edges and use a floured fork to crimp. To fry, heat oil in the deep fryer to 350°. Fry turnovers in batches until dough is puffy and filling is hot through the center. Do not rush; turnovers should bob in the oil and brown slowly. It will take about 5 minutes. Drain on paper towels. These may be kept warm in a 200° oven.

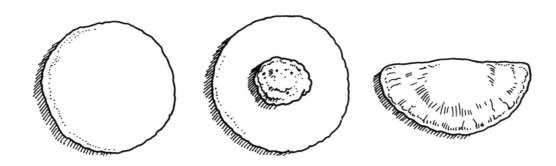

EMPANADAS

These are full of interesting flavors and textures.

½ lb. spicy sausage
1 onion, chopped
2 cloves garlic, minced
1 tsp. chili powder
1 tsp. ground cumin
1 tsp. paprika
½ tsp. unsweetened cocoa
1 tsp. sugar

1 tsp. salt
½ cup tomato paste
1 cup golden raisins
2 hard-cooked eggs, chopped
½ cup sliced green olives with
   pimientos
1 recipe *Oil Pastry*, page 34

In a large skillet, combine sausage, onion, garlic, chili powder, cumin, paprika, cocoa, sugar and salt; cook until meat is cooked and onion is soft. Drain off any excess liquid. Add tomato paste and raisins and simmer for 5 minutes. Stir in eggs and olives. Proceed with instructions for *Oil Pastry*.

MINIATURE PROSCUITTO AND CHEESE CALZONES

These make a delicious snack while watching football games in the fall.

1 lb. ricotta cheese
½ lb. mozzarella cheese, finely diced
½ cup prepared pesto
8 oz. proscuitto, finely chopped
½ cup freshly grated Parmesan cheese
salt and pepper
1 recipe *Oil Pastry*, page 34

   In a bowl, combine ricotta, mozzarella, pesto, proscuitto and Parmesan. Stir well to combine ingredients. Taste and add salt and pepper as needed. Proceed with instructions for *Oil Pastry*.

MINIATURE PIZZA CALZONES

You can use crumbled Italian sausage, or diced pepperoni or salami for the meat, or create your own original recipes.

1 lb. ricotta cheese
½ lb. mozzarella cheese, finely diced
1 small onion, chopped
¼ cup chopped green bell pepper
¼ cup chopped black olives
1 clove garlic, minced
⅓ cup grated Parmesan cheese
8 oz. meat of choice
salt and pepper
1 recipe *Oil Pastry*, page 34

In a medium bowl, combine ricotta, mozzarella, onion, green pepper, olives, garlic, Parmesan and meat; mix well. Add salt and pepper. Proceed with instructions for *Oil Pastry*.

MINIATURE VEGETABLE CALZONES

Use either broccoli or spinach in this recipe.

1 lb. ricotta cheese
½ lb. Monterey Jack cheese, finely diced
1 cup chopped cooked broccoli or spinach
2 cloves garlic, minced
½ cup chopped red bell pepper
½ cup chopped yellow bell pepper
½ cup minced fresh parsley
½ cup grated Parmesan cheese
salt and pepper
1 recipe *Oil Pastry*, page 34

In a large bowl, combine ricotta and Jack cheeses. Squeeze broccoli or spinach very dry in a cotton dish towel. Add to cheese mixture with garlic, chopped peppers, parsley and Parmesan. Mix well. Season to taste. Proceed with instructions for *Oil Pastry*.

VEGETABLE CHIPS

It's fun to use an assortment of vegetables: sweet potatoes, yams, parsnips, turnips or rutabagas. These will stay fresh for a week when stored in an airtight container. Although they are good plain, try sprinkling with a bit of salt, seasoned salt, pepper, curry or chili powder. Root vegetables can also be used to make shoestring fries, but they must be served immediately after frying.

2 lb. root vegetables
oil for deep frying
seasoning, as desired

Peel vegetables, removing any blemishes or soft spots. Using the slicing blade of a food processor or by hand using a very sharp knife, trim one end flat and thinly slice vegetables. Heat oil in the deep fryer to 370°. Fry vegetables in batches until crisp and golden, about 1 to 2 minutes. Separate any slices that stick together. Times will vary depending on thickness of slices; test one to make sure they are done. Drain on paper towels and sprinkle with seasoning of your choice.

PASTA CRISPS

These are fun for snacks and kids love them. Vary the different shapes of pasta; try lasagna noodles, rotini, bow ties or different flavored pastas, such as spinach or garlic and basil. These keep well at room temperature for 1 week. Store in an airtight container. Freeze for longer storage.

1 lb. pasta, cooked and drained
oil for deep frying
1 pkg. (1.5-2 oz.) dry salad dressing mix, such as Italian or ranch

Cook pasta as directed on package. Drain well. Spread on paper towels in a single layer and use another paper towel to blot excess moisture. Heat oil in the deep fryer to 370°. Fry cooked noodles in batches until golden brown on both sides, about 5 minutes. Drain well on paper towels. Take care that they do not stick together. Place dry salad dressing mix in a heavy plastic bag; shake with noodles to coat lightly.

BANANA CHIPS

Use green-tipped bananas to make this recipe. They make great snacks for kids.

2 bananas, peeled
oil for deep frying
salt, cinnamon sugar or powdered sugar

Cut bananas diagonally into 1/4-inch-thick slices. Heat oil in the deep fryer to 360°. Fry banana slices in batches until they begin to brown, about 1 to 2 minutes. Remove from fryer and drain on paper towels. Sprinkle with salt, cinnamon sugar or powdered sugar. Serve warm.

FRIED PARSLEY

A real conversation piece —why not make some deep fried parsley the next time you have your fryer going? It makes a tasty garnish. Because parsley has so much moisture, be prepared for it to splatter. Use to garnish main dishes, such as meats, chicken or fish.

1 bunch fresh parsley
oil for deep frying
1 tsp. salt

Divide parsley into sprigs and remove long stems. Wash and dry very thoroughly. Heat oil in the deep fryer to 370°. Drop parsley into hot oil and fry for just 5 seconds or so, until it stops sizzling. Remove from fryer and drain on paper towels. Sprinkle with salt.

FRIED SHALLOTS

These make a wonderful accompaniment to steak. Shallots are a member of the lily family and are used extensively in French cooking. They have a wonderful, mellow flavor and taste a bit like an onion with garlic.

oil for deep frying
4 oz. shallots, peeled
1 tsp. salt

Heat oil in the deep fryer to 370°. Deep fry shallots for 1 minute or until golden. Drain on paper towels. Sprinkle with salt.

FRIED RADICCHIO

If you want to be "trendy," then this is the recipe for you! It can be served as a garnish or a vegetable. Celery leaves can also be prepared in this fashion.

3 or 4 heads radicchio
oil for deep frying
salt and pepper

Trim cores from radicchio heads. Open leaves and rinse. Pat very dry with paper towels. Using a sharp knife, cut into fine shreds. Heat oil in the deep fryer to 360°. Quickly dip radicchio into hot oil for just a few seconds. Drain well on paper towels. Sprinkle with salt and pepper.

SWEET POTATO SLICES

These make an unusual appetizer; use your imagination to create different toppings.

1 lb. sweet potatoes, about 3, 2-inch
   diameter
oil for deep frying

salt and pepper
1 cup sour cream

TOPPINGS

sliced green onions
crumbled cooked bacon
crumbled cooked sausage
finely chopped crystallized ginger

chutney
apricot jam
marmalade

Scrub potatoes and trim ends off, but do not peel. Cut into ¼-inch-thick rounds. Heat oil in the deep fryer to 360°. Fry potatoes in batches until golden and cooked through, about 3 minutes. Drain on paper towels. Sprinkle lightly with salt and pepper. Cool slightly and top each round with a dollop of sour cream and one or more toppings of your choice.

DEEP FRIED TORTELLINI

It's fun to try different types of tortellini and sauces to create your own original creations. Besides the usual cheese tortellini, check your grocer's shelves for walnut and Gorgonzola, pesto, mushroom, spinach, chicken and rosemary, or beef tortellini. For sauces, try fresh tomato, spaghetti, pesto, Alfredo, red bell pepper cream sauce or a cold dip, such as sour cream and garlic with fresh herbs.

2 pkg. (9 oz. each) fresh or frozen tortellini
oil for deep frying
freshly grated Parmesan cheese, optional
sauce, as desired

Cook tortellini as directed on package. Rinse with cool water, drain and pat very dry with paper towels. Heat oil in the deep fryer to 350°. Deep fry tortellini in batches until golden, about 2 to 3 minutes. Drain on paper towels. Sprinkle with Parmesan, if desired. Spear each tortellini with a toothpick and serve with sauce of your choice.

APPETIZERS

CAJUN CHICKEN BITES

Servings: 8 as an appetizer;
4 as a main dish

You can leave the chicken breasts in halves and serve this as an entrée as well.

1 tbs. cayenne pepper
2 tbs. paprika
2 tbs. garlic powder
1 tbs. dried thyme leaves
1 tbs. dried oregano leaves
1 tbs. onion powder
1 tbs. salt

½ tsp. white pepper
½ tsp. pepper
1 cup flour
4 whole chicken breasts, skinned,
    boned and cut into 1-inch cubes
oil for deep frying

In a small bowl, combine spices, stirring well with a fork. Place seasoning mixture with flour in a plastic bag. Place chicken in bag, in batches, and shake until evenly coated. Heat oil in the deep fryer to 375°. Deep fry chicken in batches until golden brown, about 3 minutes. Drain on paper towels. Serve hot.

HAM BALLS WITH JEZEBEL SAUCE

Jezebel Sauce is a old time Southern favorite that is good with pork or roast beef. It keeps well and is a nice gift from your kitchen.

1 lb. cooked ham, finely chopped
1½ lb. pork sausage
1 small onion, finely chopped
2 cups breadcrumbs
2 eggs, beaten

½ cup milk
1 tbs. brown sugar, firmly packed
1 tsp. dry mustard
oil for deep frying
Jezebel Sauce, follows

In a large bowl, combine ham, sausage, onion, breadcrumbs, eggs, milk, brown sugar and mustard, mixing well. Shape into 1-inch balls. Heat oil in the deep fryer to 360°. Fry ham balls in batches until crispy brown and cooked through, about 3 to 4 minutes. Drain on paper towels. Keep warm in a low oven on a paper towel-lined cookie sheet. Serve with *Jezebel Sauce*.

JEZEBEL SAUCE

1 jar (18 oz.) pineapple preserves
1 jar (18 oz.) apple jelly
½ cup horseradish

3 tbs. dry mustard
1 tbs. cracked pepper

Combine all ingredients, cover and chill. Makes 4 cups.

SAUERKRAUT BALLS

These make a nice appetizer for a German meal or Oktoberfest party.

½ lb. pork sausage
¼ cup chopped onion
1 can (14 oz.) sauerkraut, well drained
2 tbs. fine dry breadcrumbs
3 oz. cream cheese
2 tbs. chopped fresh parsley
1 tsp. mustard

1 tsp. garlic salt
½ tsp. pepper
¼ cup flour
2 eggs, beaten
¼ cup milk
1 cup breadcrumbs
oil for deep frying

In a skillet, cook sausage and onion until meat is browned. Drain off any excess fat. In a large bowl, combine sausage mixture, sauerkraut, 2 tbs. breadcrumbs, cream cheese, parsley, mustard, garlic salt and pepper. Chill for several hours. Shape mixture into 1-inch balls. Place flour in a shallow bowl. In another shallow bowl, combine eggs and milk. Place 1 cup breadcrumbs in a third shallow bowl. Roll balls in flour, dip into egg mixture and dip into breadcrumbs. Heat oil in the deep fryer to 375°. Fry balls until crisp and golden and cooked through, about 4 to 5 minutes. Drain well on paper towels. Serve hot.

ARTICHOKE BALLS

Depending on how big you make these balls, this recipe makes 4 to 6 dozen. They can be made ahead, frozen and fried just before serving.

1 can (14 oz.) artichoke hearts, drained
1 cup seasoned breadcrumbs
2 tbs. olive oil
1 tbs. lemon juice
2 tbs. grated Parmesan cheese
2 eggs
2 cloves garlic, minced
1 cup grated Parmesan cheese
oil for deep frying

In a food processor or blender, combine artichoke hearts, breadcrumbs, olive oil, lemon juice, 2 tbs. Parmesan, eggs and garlic. Using your hands, roll mixture into small balls, about ¾-inch diameter. Roll in 1 cup Parmesan. Place on a cookie sheet and chill for 1 hour. Heat oil in the deep fryer to 360°. Fry balls in batches until crispy and brown. Drain on paper towels. Serve hot.

SAVORY SPINACH BALLS

Makes: 2 dozen

Serve these with sour cream mixed with a bit of Dijon mustard for dunking. For extra flavor, make the breadcrumbs out of stuffing mix.

1 pkg. (10 oz.) frozen chopped spinach, thawed
2 tbs. butter
½ cup chopped onion
1 clove garlic, minced
1 cup seasoned breadcrumbs
½ cup grated Parmesan cheese

1 egg, beaten
3 oz. cream cheese, room temperature
1 tsp. salt
½ tsp. pepper
dash Tabasco Sauce
oil for deep frying

Place spinach in a towel and squeeze dry. In a small saucepan, melt butter and sauté onion and garlic until soft. In a large bowl, combine spinach, onion mixture, breadcrumbs, Parmesan, egg, cream cheese and seasonings. Stir until thoroughly combined. Shape into 1-inch balls and chill for 1 hour. Heat oil in the deep fryer to 360°. Fry spinach balls in batches until golden brown, about 2 to 3 minutes. Drain well on paper towels. These may be kept warm in a low oven on a paper towel-lined cookie sheet. Serve hot.

ONION BALLS

*These savory appetizers are good dipped in ranch dressing, **Cocktail Sauce**, page 87, or **Mustard Dip**, page 85.*

2 tbs. butter
1½ cups finely chopped Spanish onion
2¾ cups buttermilk baking mix
½ cup beer
1 tsp. dried dill weed
oil for deep frying
1 cup shredded Parmesan cheese

In a large skillet, melt butter and sauté onion until soft; combine with baking mix, beer and dill weed. Mix well to form a stiff dough. Shape into ¾-inch balls. Heat oil in the deep fryer to 375°. Fry in batches until deep golden brown and cooked through the center, about 3 minutes. Drain on paper towels. Roll in Parmesan. Serve hot.

HAWAIIAN MEATBALLS

*To save time, use strained peach baby food for the peaches in the sauce. You can also use ground chicken or turkey in this recipe. **Peach Sauce** is also good as a glaze on spareribs or chicken wings.*

1 lb. lean ground pork
¼ cup finely chopped water chestnuts
2 green onions, finely chopped
1 egg, beaten
½ cup fine dry breadcrumbs
½ tsp. salt
¼ tsp. pepper
oil for deep frying
Peach Sauce, follows

In a bowl, combine pork, water chestnuts, onions, egg, breadcrumbs, salt and pepper until well mixed. Shape into small meatballs, about ¾-inch diameter. Heat oil in the deep fryer to 360°. Fry meatballs in batches until golden and cooked through, about 3 to 4 minutes. Drain well on paper towels. Serve hot with *Peach Sauce*.

PEACH SAUCE

1 cup canned pureed peaches
1/3 cup ketchup
1/3 cup rice vinegar
2 tbs. soy sauce
1/2 cup brown sugar, firmly packed
1 clove garlic, minced
2 tsp. ground ginger

In a saucepan, combine ingredients. Cook over medium heat, stirring occasionally, until thickened and bubbly. Store in the refrigerator in a covered container. Makes 2 cups.

CURRIED TURKEY BALLS
WITH CRANBERRY CHUTNEY

These make a delightful holiday appetizer.

1 lb. ground turkey
½ cup fine dry breadcrumbs
¼ cup finely chopped green onions
¼ cup chopped toasted slivered
   almonds
1 egg, beaten
1 tsp. salt

½ tsp. white pepper
1 tsp. curry powder
2 drops Tabasco Sauce
1 cup fine dry breadcrumbs
oil for deep frying
Cranberry Chutney, follows

In a large bowl, combine turkey, ½ cup breadcrumbs, onions, almonds, egg and seasonings. Form into small balls, about 1-inch diameter. Pour 1 cup breadcrumbs into a shallow dish. Roll balls in breadcrumbs. Heat oil in the deep fryer to 350°. Fry balls in batches until browned and cooked through, about 3 minutes. Drain on paper towels. These may be kept warm in a low oven on a paper towel-lined cookie sheet. Serve warm with *Cranberry Chutney.*

CRANBERRY CHUTNEY

1 pkg. (12 oz.) fresh cranberries
2 cups sugar
1 cup water
1 can (11 oz.) crushed pineapple,
  drained

1 cup raisins
1 tsp. cinnamon
½ tsp. allspice
½ tsp. cloves
½ tsp. nutmeg

In a large saucepan, combine cranberries, sugar and water. Bring to a boil and cook until berries start to pop. Add remaining ingredients, turn heat to low and cook until thickened. Makes 3 cups.

COCONUT PRAWNS
WITH SPICY MARMALADE

Servings: 6

The flavor and texture contrasts in this excellent appetizer make great party fare. You'll find them hard to resist. Fortunately, they can be prepared in advance and kept refrigerated until the final frying.

1 cup flour
1 tsp. salt
1 tsp. onion powder
1 tsp. garlic powder
1 tsp. paprika
½ tsp. white pepper
½ tsp. cayenne pepper
2 eggs, separated

¾ cup beer
½ cup flour
2 lb. large prawns, shelled, deveined
   and tails left intact
3 cups shredded coconut
oil for deep frying
Spicy Marmalade, follows

In a medium bowl, combine 1 cup flour, salt, onion powder, garlic powder, paprika, white pepper and cayenne. Whisk in egg yolks and beer. In a separate bowl, beat egg whites until stiff; fold into beer batter. Place ½ cup flour in a shallow bowl. Dip prawns into flour and coat well. Dip prawns into beer batter. Place coconut in a shallow bowl and roll batter-coated prawns in coconut. At this point, these may be placed on a cookie sheet, covered with plastic wrap and refrigerated for up to 8 hours. To fry, heat oil in the deep fryer to 350°. Fry prawns in batches until deep golden brown, about 2 to 4 minutes. Drain on paper towels. Serve hot with *Spicy Marmalade*.

SPICY MARMALADE

1 cup orange marmalade
3 tbs. Dijon mustard
2 tbs. horseradish
1 tsp. grated ginger root

Combine ingredients. Makes 1 cup.

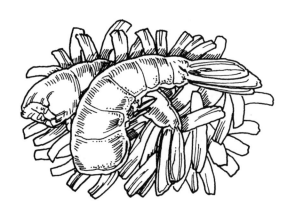

CHINESE CHICKEN SALAD

This is the only salad recipe in this book! Use your deep fryer to quickly fry the Mai Fun noodles. Mai Fun noodles are made out of rice and look like a package of brittle threads. Available in the Oriental food section of the grocery store, when fried these puff up immediately into huge billows of white, crispy noodles. Be sure to let your children watch the fun. Mirin is a seasoned rice wine; look for it in the Oriental food section, also. Be sure to read this recipe through. Although it seems long, it can be accomplished in many parts over several days. The day before you plan to serve the salad, cook the noodles and store them at room temperature.

Dressing, follows
oil for deep frying
1 pkg. (8 oz.) Mai Fun noodles
1/4 cup soy sauce
2 tbs. mirin
2 tbs. sugar
2 cloves garlic, minced
1/4 tsp. ground ginger

3 whole chicken breasts, boned, skinned and cut into 1-inch cubes
1 tbs. vegetable oil
1 large head romaine lettuce, washed and torn into bite-sized pieces
4 green onions, thinly sliced
3 tbs. toasted sesame seeds
1 cup sliced toasted almonds

Prepare *Dressing*, cover and refrigerate.

Heat oil in the deep fryer to 370°. Break noodles into 4 sections. Add one section at a time to hot oil. Noodles will immediately puff up and turn white; it just takes a second or two. Remove from fryer and drain on paper towels. Repeat with remaining noodles; set aside. In a small bowl, combine soy sauce, mirin, sugar, garlic and ginger. Stir in chicken cubes and marinate for several hours or overnight. In a large skillet over medium high heat, heat 1 tbs. vegetable oil. Remove chicken from marinade and add to skillet. Cook, stirring, until chicken is cooked through, about 3 minutes. Remove and set aside. Place romaine, onions, chicken and Mai Fun noodles in a very large salad bowl. Toss well. Drizzle with *Dressing* and add toasted sesame seeds and almonds. Toss thoroughly to coat and serve immediately.

DRESSING

¼ cup vegetable oil
¼ cup rice vinegar
2 tbs. lemon juice

6 tbs. sugar
¼ tsp. pepper

Using a food processor or blender, combine all ingredients.

WALNUT SESAME CHICKEN
WITH TANGY SWEET SAUCE

The chicken strips and sauce may be done a day ahead. You can fry the chicken just before serving.

1 lb. chicken breasts, boned and skinned
1 egg white
1 tsp. salt
2 tbs. cornstarch
1 cup walnuts
5 tbs. untoasted sesame seeds
oil for deep frying
Tangy Sweet Sauce, follows

Slice chicken into ½-inch strips across the grain. In a small bowl, combine egg white, salt and cornstarch. Add chicken and stir to coat well; set aside. Using a food processor or blender, chop walnuts and sesame seeds; place in a shallow bowl. Coat chicken with walnut mixture and place strips on a cookie sheet. Cover with plastic wrap and chill for 1 hour or up to 24 hours. To fry, heat oil in the deep fryer to 360°. Fry chicken strips in batches. Drain on paper towels. Serve warm with sauce.

TANGY SWEET SAUCE

1 tbs. oil
1 tsp. minced garlic
1 tsp. minced ginger root
2 tsp. cornstarch
2 tbs. water
3 tbs. rice vinegar
2 tbs. honey
2 tsp. soy sauce
2 tbs. tomato paste or ketchup
1/2 cup hot water

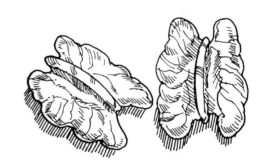

Heat a small saucepan over high heat for 30 seconds. Add oil and reduce heat to medium. Add garlic and ginger root and allow to sizzle for 1 minute; do not brown. Combine cornstarch with 2 tbs. water, and set aside. Add vinegar, honey, soy sauce, tomato paste (or ketchup) and hot water to garlic mixture and bring to a boil. Stir in cornstarch mixture and cook until mixture thickens. Makes 1 cup.

GARLIC CHICKEN WINGS WITH GINGER PEACH SAUCE

You can use peach junior baby food in this recipe to save time. This sauce is also good on spareribs.

BATTER

½ cup flour
¼ cup cornstarch
½ tsp. garlic powder
½ tsp. baking soda

¼ tsp. baking powder
¼ tsp. rice vinegar
¼ tsp. soy sauce
¾ cup water

oil for deep frying
2 lb. chicken wings
Ginger Peach Sauce, follows

Combine batter ingredients until smooth. Heat oil in the deep fryer to 375°. Dip chicken wings in batter and fry in batches until golden brown and cooked through, about 3 minutes. Drain well on paper towels. These may be kept warm in a low oven. Serve warm with *Ginger Peach Sauce*.

GINGER PEACH SAUCE

1 cup canned pureed peaches or peach baby food
1/3 cup ketchup
1/3 cup cider vinegar
2 tbs. soy sauce
1/2 cup brown sugar, firmly packed
1 clove garlic, crushed
1 tbs. grated ginger root

In a saucepan, combine ingredients and cook until thickened and bubbly. Makes 1 1/2 cups.

HONEY CHICKEN WINGS

Club soda in the batter makes it exceptionally light and crispy. These are good deep fried in peanut oil.

1/4 cup honey
1/4 cup soy sauce
1 clove garlic, minced
2 tsp. grated ginger root
2 lb. chicken wings
1 cup flour
1/2 tsp. salt
2 eggs, beaten
1 cup club soda
oil for deep frying
Honey Teriyaki Sauce, follows

In a large bowl, combine honey, soy sauce, garlic and ginger. Add chicken wings and marinate for several hours or overnight. In a bowl, combine flour, salt, eggs and club soda until smooth. Heat oil in the deep fryer to 350°. Remove wings from marinade and blot dry with paper towels. Dip into batter and fry in batches until golden brown, about 3 to 4 minutes. Drain well on paper towels. These may be kept warm in a low oven on a paper towel-lined cookie sheet. Serve hot with *Honey Teriyaki Sauce*.

HONEY TERIYAKI SAUCE

1 cup honey
½ cup soy sauce
3 tbs. ketchup
1 clove garlic, minced
2 tsp. grated ginger root

In a small saucepan, combine ingredients and heat, stirring constantly, until mixture is smooth and bubbly. Makes 1½ cups.

BUFFALO CHICKEN WINGS

Servings: 4-6

*These popular appetizers originated in Buffalo, New York. They are traditionally served with celery sticks and **Blue Cheese Dip**. My preference is to use a hot pepper sauce other than Tabasco because the flavor is too harsh. Adjust the heat to suit your personal taste. Frozen chicken wings are readily available, but do not use whole wings — only the first and second joint. Discard the tips or save them for stock.*

4 lb. chicken wings
salt and pepper
oil for deep frying
1/4 cup butter
2-5 tbs. hot pepper sauce
1 tbs. white vinegar
Blue Cheese Dip, follows
celery sticks

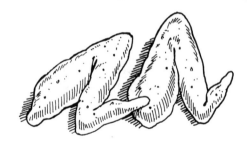

Sprinkle wings with salt and pepper. Heat oil in the deep fryer to 375°. Fry wings in batches until crispy and cooked through, about 10 minutes. Drain on paper towels and keep warm in a low oven. In a saucepan, melt butter; add hot sauce and vinegar. Pour over wings and toss to coat thoroughly. Serve hot with *Blue Cheese Dip* and celery sticks.

BLUE CHEESE DIP

1 cup mayonnaise
1 clove garlic, minced
2 tbs. finely chopped onion
1/4 cup finely chopped fresh parsley
1/2 cup sour cream
1 tbs. lemon juice
1 tsp. white vinegar
1/3 cup crumbled blue cheese
dash cayenne pepper
salt and pepper

Combine ingredients. Cover and chill for 1 hour for the flavors to mellow. Makes 1 1/2 cups.

CHICKEN AND BACON TIDBITS

Large, fresh prawns can also be used in this recipe. It's very hard to eat just one!

4 chicken breasts, boned, skinned and
   cut into 1-inch pieces
12 pieces bacon, cut into thirds
1 egg
1 cup milk
½ cup water
1 cup flour
1 tbs. cornstarch
1 tbs. sugar
2 tsp. salt
1½ tsp. baking powder
oil for deep frying
Apricot Sauce, follows

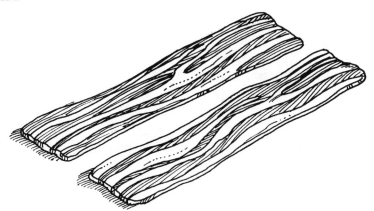

   Wrap each piece of chicken in a bacon piece and secure with a toothpick. In a bowl, combine egg, milk and water. Stir in flour, cornstarch, sugar, salt and baking powder to make a smooth batter. Heat oil in the deep fryer to 375°. Dip each chicken piece into batter. Fry in batches until crispy and golden, about 3 minutes. Test a piece to make sure it is cooked through. Drain well on paper towels. These may be kept warm in a low oven on a paper towel-lined cookie sheet. Serve hot with *Apricot Sauce*.

APRICOT SAUCE

1 cup apricot preserves
2 tbs. rice wine vinegar

Mix together and heat in a small saucepan. Serve warm. Makes 1 cup.

CRISP FRIED ARTICHOKE HEARTS WITH BÉARNAISE SAUCE

These make an excellent appetizer as is or served with another sauce, such as hollandaise sauce, tarragon-flavored mayonnaise or ranch dressing. They can be made ahead, stored in the refrigerator and fried just before serving.

1 pkg. (10 oz.) frozen artichoke hearts
1 egg, beaten
pinch salt
4 slices firm white bread
1 clove garlic, minced

¼ cup grated Parmesan cheese
4 sprigs fresh parsley
oil for deep frying
Easy Béarnaise Sauce, follows

Thaw artichoke hearts, cut in half and pat dry with paper towels. In a small bowl, combine egg with salt. Using a food processor or blender, combine bread, garlic, Parmesan and parsley to make crumbs. Place crumbs in a shallow dish. Dip each artichoke heart into egg mixture, and roll in crumbs. Heat oil in the deep fryer to 360°. Fry artichokes in batches until crispy and golden. Drain on paper towels. If not serving immediately, keep warm in a low oven on a paper towel-lined cookie sheet. Serve with *Easy Béarnaise Sauce.*

EASY BÉARNAISE SAUCE

2 tbs. white wine vinegar
2 tbs. dry white wine
1 tbs. chopped shallots
1 tsp. dried tarragon
3 egg yolks
½ cup butter
½ tsp. salt
¼ tsp. white pepper

In a small saucepan, combine vinegar, wine, shallots and tarragon. Bring to a boil and cook until reduced by half (the liquid will simmer away and the flavor will intensify). Remove from heat and cool. In a food processor or blender, process egg yolks. In another saucepan, heat butter until bubbly; slowly add to egg yolks in a slow steady stream. Add shallot mixture and season to taste. Makes 1½ cups.

SWEET AND TANGY DIPPING SAUCE

*This is excellent with shrimp, pork balls or **Cajun Chicken Bites**, page 50.*

1 cup drained chopped canned plum tomatoes
1 cup grape jelly
2/3 cup orange juice
3 tbs. lemon juice
2 cloves garlic, minced
1/2 cup golden raisins
1 jalapeño pepper, seeded and finely chopped
1 tsp. minced ginger root
1 tsp. soy sauce

In a saucepan, combine ingredients and bring to a boil, stirring constantly. Reduce heat and simmer for 10 minutes.

POSH POTATOES

These tasty morsels can be made in advance, refrigerated and reheated in a 400° oven for 10 minutes just before serving. Rinse the caviar in a sieve before using as a topping.

16 small red potatoes
oil for deep frying

1 cup sour cream

TOPPINGS
cooked crumbled bacon
sliced green onions
shredded cheese
cooked sausage

sliced olives
salsa
chopped fresh cilantro
caviar

Preheat oven to 400°. Pierce each potato with a fork. Bake potatoes for about 40 minutes or until soft when squeezed. Cool potatoes. Cut potatoes in half and scoop a small bit of potato out of the center of each using a melon baller or grapefruit spoon. Heat oil in the deep fryer to 360°. Fry potatoes in batches until crispy and golden. Drain on paper towels. Fill with each with a dollop of sour cream and topping of your choice. Serve immediately.

PECAN-CRUSTED CAMEMBERT
WITH CURRIED CRANBERRY SAUCE

Servings: 8

This makes an elegant and unusual appetizer around holiday time. Extra sauce can be stored in the refrigerator and served with your Thanksgiving turkey.

1 wheel (8 oz.) Camembert cheese
2 tbs. flour
1 egg, beaten
¼ cup finely ground pecans
1 cup fine dry breadcrumbs
oil for deep frying
Curried Cranberry Sauce, follows

Cut Camembert into 8 equal wedges, leaving white rind on cheese. Dip each wedge into flour and into beaten egg. In a shallow dish, combine pecans and breadcrumbs. Roll each cheese wedge in breadcrumb mixture to coat thoroughly. Place on a cookie sheet and freeze for at least 1 hour. Heat oil in the deep fryer to 360°. Fry cheese in batches until just crusty, about 1 minute. Drain on paper towels and serve with *Curried Cranberry Sauce*.

CURRIED CRANBERRY SAUCE

1 can (16 oz.) whole berry cranberry sauce
1/2 cup chopped pecans
2 tbs. Major Grey chutney or similar chutney
2 tsp. curry powder

In a saucepan, heat cranberry sauce to boiling. Remove from heat and add remaining ingredients. Cover and chill.

FRIED GRITS BITS

Makes: about 3 dozen

If you are crazy about grits, you are going to love this recipe. Using processed cheese instead of natural seems to give these a creamier texture. Feel free to add whatever you like to embellish this recipe — sautéed onions, ham, green chiles, bacon, sautéed red or green bell peppers, etc.

4 cups water
1 cup quick-cooking grits
1 tsp. seasoned salt
8 oz. processed American cheese
1 egg, slightly beaten

2 cloves garlic, minced
dash cayenne pepper, optional
1 cup flour
oil for deep frying
flour

In a saucepan, bring water to a boil, stir in grits and salt, and cook until thickened. Remove from heat and stir in cheese, egg, garlic, cayenne and 1 cup flour. Make sure cheese is melted and mixture is smooth. Pour into a shallow pan; grits should be no more than ½-inch thick. Refrigerate overnight. When ready to fry, heat oil in the deep fryer to 360°. Remove grits from refrigerator and, with a sharp knife, cut grits into ¾-inch squares. Shake them in flour, a few at a time, to coat. Fry until golden, about 2 minutes. Remove to paper towels to drain. Serve hot.

HAM AND SWISS PUFFS

Here's a savory hors d'oeuvre which can be made ahead and frozen. Reheat on a cookie sheet at 350° for 5 to 10 minutes, until just heated through.

6 oz. Swiss cheese, grated
½ cup finely chopped ham
2 tbs. finely chopped fresh chives
1 tbs. Dijon mustard

dash Tabasco Sauce
3 egg whites
1 cup fine dry breadcrumbs
oil for deep frying

In a medium bowl, combine cheese, ham, chives, mustard and Tabasco. In a separate bowl, beat egg whites until stiff. Stir a large spoonful of egg whites into ham and cheese mixture to "lighten" it. Gently fold in remaining egg whites just to combine. Place breadcrumbs in a shallow dish. Drop ham mixture by spoonfuls into breadcrumbs and form into round balls. Place balls on a cookie sheet and chill for 30 minutes. Heat oil in the deep fryer to 370°. Fry balls in batches until crispy and golden, about 2 minutes. Do not overcook or they will collapse. Drain on paper towels and serve hot. These may be kept warm in a 200° oven.

GARLIC PESTO CHEESE PUFFS

This special appetizer is from the Garlic Festival in Gilroy, California.

1 cup flour
1 tbs. sugar
1 tsp. baking powder
1 tsp. dried parsley
1 lb. ricotta cheese
10 cloves garlic, minced
2 tbs. prepared pesto
oil for deep frying
½ cup grated Parmesan cheese

In a large mixing bowl, combine flour, sugar, baking powder, parsley, ricotta, garlic and pesto. Stir to make a smooth batter. Heat oil in the deep fryer to 375°. Drop batter by teaspoonfuls into hot oil. Fry in batches until golden brown and puffed, about 3 minutes. Drain well on paper towels. Sprinkle with Parmesan cheese. Serve hot.

PARMESAN PUFFS

These simply elegant and delicious cheese puffs literally melt in your mouth. Serve them on a silver tray with a paper lace doily and accompany them with a nice white wine to make a charming appetizer for a dinner party.

4 egg whites
1/4 tsp. salt
1/4 tsp. cream of tartar
2 cups freshly grated Parmesan cheese
1/8 tsp. cayenne pepper
oil for deep frying

By hand or with an electric mixer, beat egg whites with salt until foamy. Add cream of tartar and continue beating until stiff peaks form. Fold in Parmesan and cayenne. Heat oil in the deep fryer to 370°. Drop batter by teaspoonfuls into hot oil. Fry in batches until golden brown, about 3 to 4 minutes. Drain on paper towels. Serve hot.

MOZZARELLA PUFFS

Don't use fresh or water-packed mozzarella for this recipe; it must be made with the dry-packaged cheese. For a variation, try adding some finely chopped sun-dried tomatoes. These may be frozen for future use after frying.

6 oz. mozzarella cheese, grated
½ cup finely chopped Italian salami
1 clove garlic, minced
½ tsp. white pepper

3 egg whites
1 cup fine dry breadcrumbs
oil for deep frying

In a medium bowl, combine cheese, salami, garlic and pepper. In a separate bowl, beat egg whites until stiff. Stir a large spoonful of egg whites into ham and cheese mixture to "lighten" it. Gently fold in remaining egg whites just to combine. Place breadcrumbs in a shallow dish. Drop cheese mixture by spoonfuls into breadcrumbs and form into round balls, about 1-inch diameter. Place balls on a cookie sheet and chill for 30 minutes. Heat oil in the deep fryer to 370°. Fry balls in batches until crispy and golden, about 2 minutes. Do not overcook or they will collapse. Drain on paper towels and serve hot. These may be kept warm in a 200° oven.

PACIFIC CRAB PUFFS

Pick over crabmeat for shells before using.

1½ cups biscuit mix
⅓ cup grated Parmesan cheese
⅓ cup finely chopped green onion
½ lb. crabmeat
1 egg, slightly beaten

⅓ cup water
dash Tabasco Sauce
oil for deep frying
Mustard Dip, follows

Combine biscuit mix, cheese and green onion. Add crabmeat. Combine egg, water and Tabasco; stir into crab mixture. Heat oil in the deep fryer to 375°. Drop batter by teaspoonfuls into hot oil. Fry in batches until golden brown, about 2 to 3 minutes. Drain on paper towels. Keep warm in a low oven on a paper towel-lined cookie sheet. Serve warm with *Mustard Dip*.

MUSTARD DIP

½ cup sour cream
2 tbs. Dijon mustard

1 tbs. lemon juice

Combine ingredients, cover and chill. Makes ¾ cup.

OYSTER PUFFS

Servings: 12

*A bowl of **Tartar Sauce**, page 114, or **Cocktail Sauce** is the perfect accompaniment for these. The base of this recipe is the classic French pastry dough pâté au choux.*

1 cup flour
½ tsp. sugar
¼ cup butter
1 cup milk
4 eggs

1 jar (10 oz.) oysters, drained and
    chopped
oil for deep frying
Cocktail Sauce, follows

In a bowl, combine flour and sugar. In a small saucepan, heat butter and milk until butter melts. Add flour all at once and stir until mixture leaves the sides of the pan and forms a ball. Place dough in a food processor or blender and add eggs, one at a time, processing well after each addition. Remove dough to a bowl and stir in oysters. Heat oil in the deep fryer to 360°. Drop mixture by teaspoonfuls into hot oil. Fry in batches until golden brown, about 5 minutes. Drain on paper towels and serve with *Cocktail Sauce*.

COCKTAIL SAUCE

1 cup ketchup
2 tbs. horseradish
1 tbs. lemon juice
dash hot pepper sauce
1 tbs. minced onion, optional
1 tbs. minced sweet pickle, optional

In a small bowl, combine ingredients. Cover and chill. Makes 1¼ cups.

CRISPY FRIED OKRA

Servings: 4

These wonderful, crunchy little nuggets are popular down South. People might be skeptical at first, but one bite and they're hooked!

1 lb. fresh okra
2 eggs, beaten
5 dashes Tabasco Sauce
1 cup yellow cornmeal
½ tsp. salt
½-1 tsp. cayenne pepper
oil for deep frying

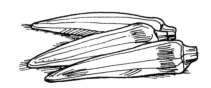

Wash okra and drain well; cut off both ends and discard. Cut okra crosswise into ½-inch slices. In a bowl, combine eggs and Tabasco; add okra and stir to coat. In a shallow dish, combine cornmeal, salt and cayenne. Dip okra pieces into cornmeal mixture to coat well. Heat oil in the deep fryer to 375°. Fry okra in batches for 5 minutes or until browned. Drain on paper towels and serve immediately.

JALAPEÑO POPPERS

These are a popular item in our local delis where they call them "poppers." They make a delicious appetizer for a Mexican meal . Serve them with salsa or blue cheese dressing for dipping.

12 jalapeño peppers, sliced in half lengthwise, seeded
8 oz. cream cheese, room temperature
2 eggs, beaten
2 tbs. water
dash salt
1 cup breadcrumbs
oil for deep frying

Fill jalapeño halves with cream cheese and press halves back together. Combine eggs, water and salt. Dip jalapeños into egg mixture and into breadcrumbs. Place on a cookie sheet and freeze for 2 hours. Heat oil in the deep fryer to 375°. Deep fry jalapeños for 2 to 3 minutes or until golden brown. Drain on paper towels.

FRIED SQUASH BLOSSOMS

An impressive appetizer, squash blossoms are often sold at produce stands or in the gourmet section of your grocer's produce department. All squash blossoms are edible and once the base forms on the female blossom, it may be removed and the squash will continue to grow. Sprinkle with grated Parmesan if desired.

20 squash blossoms
8 oz. cream cheese, room temperature
1 clove garlic, minced
2 tbs. finely chopped walnuts
1/4 cup raisins
1/2 tsp. salt
1/4 tsp. white pepper
2/3 cup flour
1 cup water
oil for deep frying

Rinse squash blossoms with cold water and pat dry. Cut off any stems. In a small bowl, combine cream cheese, garlic, nuts, raisins, salt and pepper. Spoon about 2 tsp. cream cheese mixture into the center of each blossom. Twist the top to close. Place on a cookie sheet and refrigerate for 30 minutes. In a small bowl, whisk together flour and water and allow to stand for 15 minutes. Heat oil in the deep fryer to 325°. Dip each squash blossom into flour batter and fry in batches until golden brown, about 3 minutes. Drain on paper towels. Serve warm.

AVOCADO FRITTERS

Servings: 4-8

To ripen an avocado, leave it at room temperature. When it has reached the desired ripeness, store it in the refrigerator. Ripe avocados are soft but not mushy.

2 large avocados, pitted, peeled and cut into ½-inch-thick crescents
1 tsp. garlic salt
2 eggs, beaten
1 cup evaporated milk
½ tsp. Worcestershire sauce
⅔ cup cornstarch
4 tsp. baking powder
½ tsp. salt
½ tsp. pepper
oil for deep frying

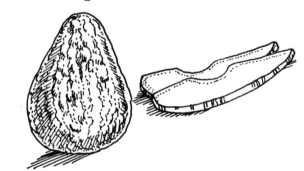

Sprinkle avocado pieces with garlic salt. In a small bowl, beat together eggs, evaporated milk and Worcestershire until smooth. Whisk in cornstarch, baking powder, salt and pepper. Heat oil in the deep fryer to 375°. Dip avocado pieces into batter. Fry in batches until deep golden brown, about 2 to 4 minutes. Drain on paper towels. Serve hot.

CALAMARI WITH AOILI
(SQUID WITH GARLIC SAUCE)

Calamari, or squid, is a delightful, mild-flavored seafood. It can be cut into rings; used as a container for stuffing; added to soups, chowders or pasta; made into steaks; or served raw as sushi. Cleaning squid is not fun, but you can buy it already cleaned and sliced at the fish market or grocery store. It is also available frozen.

1 cup flour
1 tsp. salt
1 tsp. pepper
1 tsp. paprika
2 eggs

2 cups fine dry breadcrumbs
2 lb. squid, cleaned and cut into rings
oil for deep frying
Garlic Sauce, follows

In a shallow dish, combine flour and seasonings. Place eggs and breadcrumbs in separate dishes. Dry squid thoroughly on paper towels. Dip squid into flour, egg and into breadcrumbs. Place on a paper towel-lined cookie sheet; at this point, it may be covered and stored in the refrigerator for several hours. To prepare, heat oil in the deep fryer to 375°. Fry squid in batches until light golden brown, about 2 minutes. Do not overcook or it will become tough. Drain on paper towels. Serve hot with *Garlic Sauce*.

GARLIC SAUCE

½ cup butter
4 large cloves garlic, minced
4 egg yolks
2 tbs. Dijon mustard

½ tsp. salt
¼ tsp. white pepper
dash Tabasco Sauce

In a small skillet, melt 2 tbs. butter and sauté garlic until soft but not brown. Using a food processor or blender, combine egg yolks and seasonings. In another skillet, bring remaining butter to a boil. Add garlic mixture to egg yolks; add bubbling butter. Pour into a small bowl.

CURRIED PINEAPPLE FRITTERS
WITH CHUTNEY SAUCE

These appetizers are fun to serve at a tropical luau party. A fresh pineapple will ripen more evenly if you stand it upside down. Just prop it against something and balance it on its fronds, and leave it at room temperature.

BATTER

1 cup flour
1 tsp. baking powder
2 egg yolks
½ tsp. salt

½ tsp. white pepper
½ tsp. paprika
1 tsp. curry powder
1 cup beer

2 cups fresh or canned pineapple
    chunks

oil for deep frying
Chutney Sauce, follows

In a medium bowl, combine batter ingredients and whisk until smooth. Refrigerate for 1 hour. Blot pineapple dry with paper towels. Heat oil in the deep fryer to 350°. Dip pineapple pieces into batter and slip into hot oil. Fry in batches until crisp and golden, about 2 to 3 minutes. Serve hot with *Chutney Sauce*.

CHUTNEY SAUCE

1 cup Major Grey chutney or similar chutney
½ cup melted apple jelly
1 tbs. lemon juice
2 tsp. mustard

In a food processor or blender, combine all ingredients. Heat in a small saucepan and serve warm. Makes 1½ cups.

SHRIMP TOASTS WITH SESAME SOY DIPPING SAUCE

*A savory shrimp mixture is spread on white bread for this delicious Chinese-style recipe. For variety, the **Shrimp Paste** may be used for **Won Tons**, page 97, **Crab Claws**, page 98, **Butterflied Prawns**, page 98, or **Prickly Shrimp Balls**, page 99. All of these are good with **Sesame Soy Dipping Sauce** or **Plum Sauce**, page 100.*

SHRIMP PASTE

1 lb. shrimp, shelled and deveined
2 egg whites
2 green onions, white part only, finely minced
2 tbs. grated ginger root
2 tbs. soy sauce

2 tbs. dry sherry
2 tsp. dark Oriental sesame oil
2 tbs. cornstarch
1½ tsp. salt
1 tsp. white pepper

6 slices firm white sandwich bread
oil for deep frying

Sesame Soy Dipping Sauce, follows

To make *Shrimp Paste*: Using a food processor or blender, combine shrimp and egg whites to form a smooth paste. Add onions, ginger, soy sauce, sherry, sesame oil, cornstarch, salt and pepper. Process until smooth. Refrigerate for 1 hour before using.

Spread paste evenly on bread slices. Trim crusts and cut bread into 4 triangles or 4 long fingers. Heat oil in the deep fryer to 370°. Place toasts shrimp side down into hot oil and fry until golden brown; turn to brown other side — about 3 to 4 minutes total. Drain on paper towels. Serve hot with *Sesame Soy Dipping Sauce*.

SESAME SOY DIPPING SAUCE

1 cup soy sauce
2 tbs. dark Oriental sesame oil
1 tsp. hot chile oil, or to taste

2 green onions, finely sliced
1 tbs. finely chopped ginger root

In a small bowl, combine ingredients. Store in the refrigerator. Makes 1 cup.

VARIATION: WON TONS

1 recipe *Shrimp Paste*
1 pkg. (1 lb.) won ton wrappers

oil for deep frying

Place 1 tsp. *Shrimp Paste* in the center of each won ton wrapper. Fold edge over filling and roll to within 1 inch of the corner. Moisten edges of won ton wrapper with water and fold side corners over, overlapping the points slightly. Pinch together to seal. (See diagram on page 27.) Place filled won tons in a single layer on a cookie sheet. Heat oil in the deep fryer to 350°. Fry won tons in batches until crisp and golden, about 2 minutes. Drain on paper towels. Serve warm with sauce for dipping.

VARIATION: CRAB CLAWS

12 frozen crab claws, about 3-4 inches
each, with cartilage, meat and pincers

1 recipe *Shrimp Paste*
oil for deep frying

Thaw crab claws in the refrigerator overnight. Gently squeeze claws to remove excess moisture; pat dry with paper towels. Form *Shrimp Paste* around claws, leaving pincers exposed. At this point, they can be refrigerated for 1 day. To prepare, heat oil in the deep fryer to 350°. Fry claws, a few at a time, until puffed and golden, about 3 to 5 minutes. Drain on paper towels. Serve warm with sauce for dipping.

VARIATION: BUTTERFLIED PRAWNS

1 lb. prawns, about 26 to 30, peeled
and deveined
1 recipe *Shrimp Paste*

Basic Beer Batter, page 104
oil for deep frying

To butterfly prawns, cut down center back to the tail, spreading meat open. Leave tail intact. Press 1 tbs. *Shrimp Paste* onto the top of each prawn, making an even layer.

Prepare *Basic Beer Batter*. Dip prawns into batter. Heat oil in the deep fryer to 360°. Fry prawns in batches until golden, about 2 to 3 minutes. Remove and drain on paper towels. Serve warm with sauce for dipping.

VARIATION: PRICKLY SHRIMP BALLS

¼ lb. cellophane noodles
oil for deep frying
1 recipe *Shrimp Paste*

1 cup cornstarch
1 egg white

Prepare noodles first: Heat oil in the deep fryer to 370°. Break the package of noodles into fourths. Fry one batch of noodles at a time. Drop into hot oil; noodles will immediately puff up and turn white. Remove and drain on paper towels. Repeat with remaining noodles. When noodles are cool and brittle, crush with a rolling pin and place on a rimmed cookie sheet.

Form *Shrimp Paste* into 1-inch balls. Roll in cornstarch. In a shallow bowl, beat egg white until frothy. Roll shrimp balls in egg white and dip into crushed cellophane noodles to coat. At this point, these may be refrigerated for up to 6 hours. To fry, heat oil in the deep fryer to 370°. Fry shrimp balls in batches until lightly browned and cooked through, about 3 minutes. Test one to make sure they are done. Drain on paper towels and serve warm with sauce for dipping.

PLUM SAUCE

This sauce is best made ahead so that the flavors blend for a day or so. Store in the refrigerator.

3 tsp. cornstarch
½ cup water
½ cup plum jam
⅓ cup apricot jam
3 tbs. rice vinegar
2 tsp. minced garlic
1 tsp. minced ginger root
½ tsp. salt
½ tsp. dried red pepper flakes

Dissolve cornstarch in water. In a saucepan, combine ingredients and bring to a boil. Reduce heat and simmer for 2 minutes.

SZECHWAN CHILI SAUCE

Excellent with egg rolls; spring rolls; won tons; or fried shrimp, chicken or fruit fritters. This keeps well stored in a covered container in the refrigerator. Szechwan hot bean paste should be added last, to taste. Look for it in the Oriental food section of your grocery store.

¾ cup cider vinegar
½ cup soy sauce
½ cup brown sugar, firmly packed
½ cup bottled chili sauce
1 cup crushed pineapple with juice
1 tbs. sherry
1 tsp. Worcestershire sauce
Szechwan hot bean paste

In a medium saucepan, combine all ingredients, except hot bean paste. Cook over medium heat for 5 minutes. Add a bit of bean paste and taste; add more if needed.

ENTRÉES

TIPS ON DEEP FRYING CHICKEN

- Larger pieces of chicken, such as breasts and thighs, will remain more tender and not dry out if they are simmered for 20 minutes in lightly salted water (1 tsp. salt per quart) before they are fried.

- For convenience, you can partially fry the chicken the night before serving, refrigerate overnight and finish by baking the chicken the next day.

- If your family prefers only one part, such as breasts or thighs, avoid disputes by buying only that particular piece.

- Experiment with spices and marinades. Before rolling in crumbs or batter, try marinating raw chicken in one or more of the following: buttermilk, cream, prepared salad dressings, lemon juice, oils and herbs.

- The following can all be used to make delicious and unusual combinations of coatings for chicken before frying:

breadcrumbs — plain or seasoned	crushed bouillon cubes	nuts: hazelnuts, peanuts, pecans, walnuts, etc.
coconut	crushed cereal	
cornmeal	crushed potato or taco chips	sesame seeds
cornstarch	dry salad dressing mixes	shredded Parmesan cheese
cracker crumbs	herbs	

BASIC BEER BATTER

This batter is exceptionally light, due to the yeast in the beer. Use a light beer, not a dark one, and it is perfectly acceptable if it is flat. This is excellent for chicken, fish or onion rings.

½ cup flour
½ cup cornstarch
¼ tsp. cayenne pepper
¼ tsp. garlic powder
1 egg
1 cup beer
2 tbs. oil

Combine ingredients until smooth. Cover and refrigerate for 1 hour.

BASIC CRISPY BATTER

Makes: 1½ cups

This basic batter is good on chicken, fish, meat and vegetables. Be sure to dip the food in the batter to coat thoroughly. Food may be dipped into breadcrumbs after coating with batter, if desired.

¾ cup flour
¼ cup cornstarch
2 tsp. baking powder
1 tsp. salt
1 cup water

In a medium bowl, combine dry ingredients. Whisk in water until batter is smooth.

BATTER FRIED CHICKEN

In order to get evenly fried pieces of chicken and not have them overly done or dried out, a good trick is to simmer the chicken pieces in salted water for 20 minutes to precook.

one 3 lb. frying chicken, cut into serving
  pieces
salted water
1 cup flour
1 tsp. baking powder
1 tsp. seasoned salt
1 tsp. paprika

1 tsp. garlic salt
1 tsp. pepper
½ tsp. poultry seasoning
1 egg
½ cup milk
oil for deep frying

Place chicken pieces in a large saucepan and cover with salted water. Simmer over low heat for 20 minutes. Drain well and pat dry with paper towels. In a medium bowl, combine dry ingredients. In a small bowl, beat egg and milk. Whisk into flour mixture, combining well. Heat oil in the deep fryer to 350°. Dip chicken pieces into batter, allowing excess batter to drain back into bowl. Fry chicken in batches until deep golden brown and cooked through. Juices should run clear when pierced with a fork. Drain on paper towels. Keep warm in a 200° oven while frying remaining chicken.

SPICY BUTTERMILK FRIED CHICKEN

Servings: 4

Marinate chicken overnight in buttermilk to give it extra tang and tenderness.

2 cups buttermilk
2 tsp. salt
one 3 lb. frying chicken, cut into serving
   pieces
2 cups flour
2 tsp. pepper

2 tsp. salt
2 tsp. paprika
1 tsp. cayenne pepper
1 tsp. crumbled dried thyme leaves
1 tsp. garlic powder
oil for deep frying

In a large bowl, combine buttermilk and salt. Add chicken and stir to coat thoroughly. Cover and refrigerate overnight. Combine flour and seasonings in a heavy-duty plastic bag. Remove chicken from marinade. Place chicken pieces in bag and shake to coat with flour. Place chicken on a cookie sheet. Heat oil in the deep fryer to 350°. Fry chicken, cooking dark meat (such as thighs and drumsticks) first, for 12 minutes or until crispy and golden. Drain on paper towels and keep warm in a 200° oven while preparing remaining pieces. Fry breasts and other white meat for 10 minutes, or until juices run clear when pierced with a fork.

CRISPY STUFFED CHICKEN BREASTS

Servings: 8

*Make these the day before you plan to serve them. Served with **Delicate Cheese Sauce**, they make elegant company fare.*

4 large whole chicken breasts
8 slices Black Forest ham, thinly sliced
8 green onions, tops only
1½ cups flour
1 tsp. dried tarragon
2 tsp. salt
½ tsp. pepper
1 tsp. paprika
¼ tsp. garlic powder
¼ tsp. dry mustard
½ cup milk
4 eggs, beaten
¼ tsp. salt
2 cups fine dry breadcrumbs
oil for deep frying
Delicate Cheese Sauce, follows

Bone, skin and halve chicken breasts. Place each half between two sheets of waxed paper and pound to $\frac{1}{4}$-inch thickness. Place 1 slice ham and a 2-inch piece of green onion on top of each breast. Do not allow any ham or onion to hang over sides of chicken breasts. With the shortest side toward you, roll up chicken breasts, jelly roll-style, making sure all filling is wrapped tightly inside chicken bundles. In a shallow bowl, combine flour, tarragon, 2 tsp. salt, pepper, paprika, garlic powder and mustard. In another shallow bowl, combine milk, eggs and $\frac{1}{4}$ tsp. salt. Place breadcrumbs in a third bowl. Dip chicken bundles into flour mixture, coating well. Dip into egg mixture and breadcrumbs. Place on a rack and allow to dry for 1 hour in the refrigerator. Cover with plastic wrap and keep refrigerated overnight.

Heat oil in the deep fryer to 360°. Fry breasts in batches until golden and chicken is cooked through, about 8 to 10 minutes. Drain on paper towels and keep warm in a low oven while frying remaining chicken. Serve hot with *Delicate Cheese Sauce*.

DELICATE CHEESE SAUCE

1 cup sour cream
1 cup grated cheddar cheese

$\frac{1}{2}$ cup grated Parmesan cheese
milk, as needed

In the top of a double boiler over simmering water, whisk ingredients together until cheeses are melted and sauce is smooth. Add a bit of milk to thin, if necessary.

CHICKEN KIEV

This makes a classically elegant dish for a dinner party. As guests cut into golden chicken breast bundles, they are rewarded with the delicious burst of garlic and herb-flavored butter. Serve with wild rice pilaf, baby carrots and a butter lettuce salad.

½ cup butter
2 tbs. minced fresh parsley
2 tbs. snipped fresh chives
1 clove garlic, minced
½ tsp. salt
½ tsp. pepper
1 tsp. Worcestershire sauce

8 large chicken breasts, boned, halved
  and skinned
1 cup flour
2 eggs
¾ cup milk
2 cups finely crushed Ritz crackers
oil for deep frying

In a small bowl, by hand or using a food processor or blender, cream together butter, parsley, chives, garlic, salt, pepper and Worcestershire until smoothly blended. Using plastic wrap, shape mixture into a log. Roll to make log about ¾-inch diameter. Cut into 8 equal pieces and freeze until solid. Place chicken breast halves on a cutting board and gently pound them to flatten to ¼-inch thickness. Be careful not to cut through meat. Remove butter log from freezer; place 1 piece of frozen butter mixture in the center of each pounded breast. Fold over meat to completely enclose butter. Secure with wooden toothpicks. Place flour in a shallow bowl. In another shallow bowl, combine eggs and milk. Place Ritz cracker crumbs in a third shallow bowl. Dip breasts in flour, egg mixture and crumbs. Roll to coat completely. At this point, these may be placed on a cookie sheet, covered with plastic wrap and refrigerated for up to 24 hours. To fry, heat oil in the deep fryer to 360°. Fry chicken in batches until deep golden brown, about 8 to 10 minutes. Serve immediately.

MEXICAN CHICKEN KIEV

Salsa, guacamole and sour cream are wonderful to serve with this entrée.

4 whole chicken breasts, halved, boned
    and skinned
8 oz. Monterey Jack cheese
1 can (7 oz.) diced green chiles
1 cup flour
2 eggs
½ cup milk

¾ cup dry breadcrumbs
½ cup grated Parmesan cheese
1½ tbs. chili powder
1 tsp. salt
½ tsp. ground cumin
½ tsp. pepper
oil for deep frying

Pound each breast to ¼-inch thickness; do not tear meat. Cut cheese into 8 long fingers; place 1 finger in the center of each breast. Place 1 tbs. chiles on each piece of cheese. Fold ends and sides of breast over filling; secure tightly with toothpicks. Dip breasts in flour to coat thoroughly. In a shallow dish, beat eggs and milk. In another shallow dish, combine breadcrumbs, Parmesan and spices. Dip floured breasts into egg mixture; roll in breadcrumbs to coat well. Place on a cookie sheet, cover with plastic wrap and refrigerate for 1 hour or overnight. Heat oil in the deep fryer to 350°. Fry in batches, turning to brown evenly. Fry for 5 to 7 minutes or until golden brown and cooked through. Drain on paper towels. Keep warm in a 200° oven.

FISH AND CHIPS

*In London, they always have you select the variety of fish you want with your chips. Now you can prepare this English favorite at home using your favorite kind of fish. Serve with chips (**French Fries**, page 144), **Tartar Sauce**, page 114, ketchup and malt vinegar.*

1 cup flour
1 cup beer
½ tsp. salt
2 lb. firm white fish, such as sole, cod or halibut, cut in pieces

In a medium bowl, combine flour, beer and salt, whisking until smooth. Allow to stand at room temperature for 30 minutes to allow the gluten in the flour to relax. Heat oil in the deep fryer to 370°. Dip fish pieces into batter, allowing excess to drip back into bowl. Fry fish in batches until golden brown and crispy, about 5 minutes. Drain well on paper towels. Keep warm in a 200° oven while frying remaining fish.

TARTAR SAUCE

Homemade tartar sauce just can't be beat. Adjust the recipe to suit your personal taste. Try adding dill weed or chopped green pepper. It is important to drain the chopped vegetables in a sieve so they won't be bitter. A food processor makes the preparation a breeze. This is best made at least a day ahead of time so the flavors can mellow.

½ cup finely chopped celery
½ cup finely chopped onion
¼ cup finely chopped fresh parsley
1 tsp. salt
2 cups mayonnaise
4 large dill pickles with about 1 tbs. juice

2 tsp. Worcestershire sauce
2 tbs. lemon juice
¼ tsp. Tabasco Sauce
2 cloves garlic, minced
½ tsp. pepper

With a food processor, blender or by hand, chop celery, onion and parsley. Place in a wire mesh sieve and sprinkle with salt. Allow to stand for 10 minutes; rinse with cold water and wring out excess moisture in a towel. Place mayonnaise in a bowl and add vegetable mixture. Chop pickles and add with juice to mayonnaise mixture. Stir in seasonings; taste and adjust if necessary. Spoon into an airtight container and refrigerate overnight before serving.

SESAME SCALLOPS

Use small scallops or cut large ones into quarters. Oriental dark sesame oil can be found in the Oriental food section of the grocery store. It is a flavoring oil only and is not frying oil. Serve with steamed white rice and snow peas.

1½ cups cornstarch
½ cup untoasted sesame seeds

1½ lb. scallops
oil for deep frying

SAUCE

6 tbs. lemon juice
3 tbs. orange juice
1 tbs. cornstarch

1 tbs. grated ginger root
1 tbs. Oriental dark sesame oil
1 tsp. salt

In a medium bowl, combine cornstarch and sesame seeds. Dip scallops into cornstarch mixture, coating well. Shake off any excess. Heat oil in the deep fryer to 370°. Fry scallops in batches until golden, about 2 minutes. Drain well on paper towels.

To prepare sauce: In a small bowl, whisk together lemon juice, orange juice, cornstarch, ginger, sesame oil and salt. Place a large skillet over medium high heat. Add cooked scallops and pour sauce over. Stir mixture until sauce thickens and scallops are heated through.

PANKO FRIED OYSTERS

*Panko is a type of Japanese breadcrumbs made out of rice flour. It gives a very light and delicate crispy coating to fried foods. Look for it in the Oriental food section of the grocery store. Serve with lemon wedges, ketchup and **Tartar Sauce**, page 114, for dipping.*

1 cup flour
1 tbs. dried dill weed
1 tbs. dried thyme leaves
1 tsp. salt
½ tsp. pepper

2 doz. medium oysters
1 can (12 oz.) beer
2 cups panko breadcrumbs
oil for deep frying

Combine flour, dill, thyme, salt and pepper in a plastic bag. Add oysters and shake to coat well. Dip each oyster in beer and then roll in panko breadcrumbs. Heat oil in the deep fryer to 370°. Fry oysters for 1 to 2 minutes or until crispy and golden brown. Drain on paper towels.

CORNMEAL CLAMS

*The texture and flavor of cornmeal is particularly good with clams. This recipe can also be used for oysters, scallops or shrimp. Serve with ketchup or **Tartar Sauce**, page 114.*

1½ lb. clams, shucked
⅓ cup flour
1 tsp. salt
½ tsp. pepper

2 eggs
¼ tsp. salt
dash Tabasco Sauce
1 cup yellow cornmeal

Rinse and drain clams. Pat dry with paper towels. In a shallow dish, combine flour, salt and pepper. In another shallow dish, beat eggs with salt and Tabasco. Place cornmeal in a third dish. Roll clams in seasoned flour to coat; dip in egg and in cornmeal. Place on a rack to dry and to allow coating to adhere; leave clams for about 20 minutes. Heat oil in the deep fryer to 360°. Fry clams in batches until crispy, about 2 to 3 minutes. Do not overcook or they will become tough. Drain on paper towels. Serve hot with sauce.

FRIED CATFISH

*The popular Southern favorite is now available in all parts of the United States thanks to farm-raised catfish. For an excellent menu, serve this with **Squash Puppies**, page 146, and coleslaw.*

8 whole catfish, about 4 lb., cleaned
  and dressed
2 tbs. lemon juice
2½ cups flour, divided
2 tsp. salt, divided

1 tbs. paprika
1 can (12 oz.) beer
oil for deep frying
fresh parsley and lemon wedges

Rinse fish with cold water and pat dry. Sprinkle with lemon juice. Chill for 30 minutes.

Combine 1¼ cups flour and 1 tsp. salt. Dip fish in flour mixture, coating well. Combine remaining 1¼ cups flour, 1 tsp. salt and paprika. Add beer and stir until batter is smooth. Dip fish into batter. Heat oil in the deep fryer to 375°. Fry fish in batches until fish pieces float to the surface and are golden brown on both sides. Drain on paper towels. Garnish with parsley and lemon wedges.

INTERNATIONAL SPECIALTIES

DIRECTIONS FOR SPRING ROLLS AND EGG ROLLS

There are a variety of delicious fillings in this section that can be used interchangeably to make either *Spring Rolls* or *Egg Rolls*. Egg roll wrappers are generally larger and thicker. Egg rolls are often cut into thirds for serving. In the Philippines, the wrappers are called *lumpia*. The wrappers are available in the Oriental food section or in the produce department of the grocery store. Leftover wrappers can be wrapped tightly and frozen. It is important to seal them well so excess moisture won't get in and cause them to stick together.

Prepare the filling of your choice. Mound about 2 rounded tablespoons of filling in a 3-inch strip across wrapper, about 2 inches above the lower corner. Fold bottom corner over filling and roll over once. Fold over corners. Brush all three exposed edges with beaten egg. Roll to enclose completely; the egg will seal the wrapper to itself. Place filled rolls on a cookie sheet while preparing remainder. They may be covered with plastic wrap and refrigerated overnight.

To fry: Heat oil in the deep fryer to 360°. Fry 3 to 4 rolls at a time until golden brown, about 3 minutes. Remove and drain on paper towels. These may be kept warm in a 200° oven while preparing remainder.

To freeze: Cool rolls and freeze in freezer bags or wrap tightly in heavy-duty foil. To reheat, do not thaw. Place rolls in a single layer on a cookie sheet and bake, uncovered, at 350° for 15 to 25 minutes or until hot.

THAI SPRING ROLL FILLING

Fresh cilantro gives a real burst of flavor. Thai fish sauce is called "nam pla," and if you can't find it in the Oriental food section of the grocery store, you can substitute soy sauce. Look for the cellophane noodles there as well.

2 tbs. vegetable oil
4 cloves garlic, minced
4 tbs. chopped fresh cilantro
1 pkg. (3½ oz.) cellophane noodles
1 lb. ground pork
2 eggs, beaten
½ cup finely chopped onion

2 tbs. Thai fish sauce (nam pla)
1 tsp. white pepper
2 tsp. sugar
1 tsp. salt
spring roll wrappers
egg
oil for deep frying

Heat oil in a skillet over medium high heat; add garlic and cilantro, and stir fry for 1 minute. Remove from heat. Soak cellophane noodles in warm water for 5 minutes. Drain well and cut into 2-inch lengths. In a large bowl, combine pork, eggs, onion, fish sauce, pepper, sugar and salt. Add garlic mixture and cellophane noodles, mixing well. Proceed with instructions for making *Spring Rolls*, page 120.

CRAB FILLING

Use this recipe to make expensive crabmeat go a long way.

¾ lb. fresh crabmeat
2 tsp. dry sherry
2 tsp. soy sauce
½ tsp. sugar
½ tsp. salt
1 tsp. Oriental dark sesame oil
1 tsp. cornstarch
2 tbs. vegetable oil
1 tsp. chopped ginger root

2 cups fresh bean sprouts
1 cup thinly sliced mushrooms
1 cup thinly sliced celery
¾ cup chopped bamboo shoots
3 green onions, thinly sliced
egg roll or spring roll wrappers
egg
oil for deep frying

Pick over crabmeat and remove any shell fragments or cartilage. In a small bowl, combine sherry, soy sauce, sugar, salt, sesame oil and cornstarch; set aside. In a large skillet, heat 2 tbs. oil over high heat. When it is hot, add ginger. Stir briefly to infuse oil with ginger flavor. Add bean sprouts, mushrooms, celery and bamboo shoots. Cook, stirring often, for 2 minutes. Add crabmeat, green onions and sherry mixture; cook until thickened. Remove from heat and cool. Proceed with instructions for making *Egg Rolls* or *Spring Rolls*, page 120.

CURRIED BEEF FILLING

Dip these in hot mustard, ketchup or chutney.

½ lb. lean ground beef
½ cup finely chopped onion
1 clove garlic, minced
2 tsp. curry powder
¼ tsp. salt
1 tsp. soy sauce
2 tsp. dry sherry
egg roll or spring roll wrappers
egg
oil for deep frying

Crumble ground beef into a skillet over medium high heat. Add onion and garlic; cook until beef is browned and onion is tender. Drain off any excess fat. Add curry powder, salt, soy sauce and sherry, and cook for 1 minute. Cool. Proceed with instructions for making *Egg Rolls* or *Spring Rolls*, page 120.

CHORIZO FLAUTAS

Chorizo is a highly seasoned sausage, which you can make yourself with ground pork and spices. A "flauta" is a corn tortilla that is rolled around a filling and fried until crisp. Serve flautas on a bed of shredded lettuce and top with salsa and sour cream.

1 onion, finely chopped
1 lb. lean ground pork
2 tsp. chili powder
2 tsp. crumbled fresh oregano leaves
½ tsp. ground cumin
¼ tsp. cinnamon

1 tsp. salt
½ tsp. Tabasco Sauce, optional
2 tbs. vinegar
¼ cup ketchup
12 corn tortillas
oil for deep frying

In a large skillet over medium high heat, brown onion and pork. Pour off any excess liquid. Add chili powder, oregano, cumin, cinnamon, salt, Tabasco, vinegar and ketchup. Cook mixture over medium heat until liquid is evaporated. Place tortillas on a flat surface. Spoon meat mixture into center of each tortilla in the shape of a rectangle, dividing mixture evenly. Fold over ends and sides and secure with toothpicks. Heat oil in the deep fryer to 360°. Fry tortillas in batches until golden brown, about 2 minutes. Drain on paper towels. Keep warm in a low oven while frying remainder. Serve hot.

124   INTERNATIONAL SPECIALTIES

BEAN AND BEEF CHIMICHANGAS

Use taco seasoning to save steps when preparing this Mexican dish. Serve with guacamole, sour cream and salsa.

1 lb. lean ground beef
1 small onion, chopped
1 clove garlic, minced
1 pkg. (1.5 oz.) taco seasoning mix
8 large flour tortillas, 8-inch diameter or larger
2 cups refried beans
1 cup shredded cheddar cheese
oil for deep frying

In a skillet over medium high heat, brown beef, onion and garlic. Drain off any excess fat and add taco seasoning. Place tortillas on a flat surface; spread each with 1/4 cup refried beans, 1/8 of the meat mixture and 2 tbs. cheese. Fold ends and both sides over and secure with toothpicks. Heat oil in the deep fryer to 370°. Fry chimichangas in batches until golden brown and crispy, about 2 to 3 minutes. Drain on paper towels. Serve hot.

CHICKEN AND CREAM CHEESE CHALUPAS

"Chalupa" is the Spanish word for "boat." A chalupa is a corn tortilla formed into a boat shape and fried until crisp. Serve these with salsa, sour cream and shredded cheddar cheese — a great way to use leftover chicken or turkey.

8 oz. cream cheese, room temperature
2 cups chopped cooked chicken
1 can (4 oz.) chopped green chiles
1/4 cup diced onion
8 large flour tortillas, 8-inch diameter or larger
oil for deep frying

Combine cream cheese, chicken, chiles and onion. Place tortillas on a flat surface, and spread 1/8 of the cream cheese mixture in the center of each, making a rectangular shape. Fold ends and sides over to enclose filling completely and fasten with wooden toothpicks. Heat oil in the deep fryer to 360°. Fry chalupas until golden brown and crispy, about 4 minutes. Drain on paper towels.

CHILES RELLENOS

Puffy egg batter surrounds a mild chile stuffed with Jack cheese in this traditional recipe. Serve your favorite salsa to spoon over the top.

2 cans (4 oz. each) whole green chiles
½ lb. Monterey Jack cheese
½ cup flour
3 eggs, separated

1 tbs. water
3 tbs. flour
¼ tsp. salt
oil for deep frying

Drain chiles and cut a slit down the side of each, being careful to keep chile in one piece. Gently remove seeds and membrane inside. Cut cheese into sticks, about ½-inch wide, ½-inch thick and 1 inch shorter than chiles. Place cheese inside chiles and press sides together to seal. Place ½ cup flour in a shallow dish and roll chiles in flour to coat. Place chiles on a waxed paper-lined cookie sheet and chill for 1 hour.

To prepare batter: With an electric mixer or by hand, beat egg whites until stiff. In a bowl, combine egg yolks, water, 3 tbs. flour and salt until smooth. Gently fold in egg whites. Heat oil in the deep fryer to 375°. Dip each chile into batter and place on a saucer. Slide chiles from saucer into hot oil. Fry until puffy and golden, about 4 minutes.

SWEET AND SOUR PORK

Serve this over a bed of steamed white rice.

1 lb. boneless pork loin or shoulder
1 tbs. soy sauce
1/4 cup chicken broth
1/4 cup rice vinegar
2 tbs. soy sauce

2 tsp. brown sugar, firmly packed
1/2 tsp. white pepper
2 tsp. cornstarch
1/4 cup water

BATTER

1 1/3 cups flour
1 tsp. salt
2 eggs, separated

oil for deep frying

1 tbs. oil
3/4 cup beer

SAUCE

2 tbs. oil
2 tbs. grated ginger root
2 cloves garlic, minced
3 green onions, sliced diagonally into
    1-inch pieces

1 green bell pepper, cut into 1-inch
    pieces
1 red bell pepper, cut into 1-inch pieces
1 cup pineapple chunks, in their own
    juice, drained

Cut pork into 1-inch cubes and combine with 1 tbs. soy sauce. In a medium bowl, combine chicken broth, vinegar, 2 tbs. soy sauce, brown sugar and pepper. In another bowl, dissolve cornstarch in water; combine with chicken broth mixture. Set aside for sauce. Prepare batter.

Combine flour, salt, egg yolks, oil and beer until smooth. Beat egg whites until stiff. Fold into beer mixture.

Heat oil in the deep fryer to 350°. Dip pork into batter and fry until crisp and golden, about 3 minutes. Drain on paper towels. Keep warm in a low oven. Prepare sauce.

In a large skillet, heat oil over medium high heat. Add ginger, garlic, green onions and peppers. Stir fry until tender-crisp. Add reserved chicken broth mixture and pineapple and cook until thickened and bubbly.

Pour sauce over cooked pork cubes.

LEMON CHICKEN

The secret to this dish is lime juice in the sauce. Serve over steamed white rice.

1/4 cup water
1 tbs. sherry
1/4 tsp. garlic powder
1/4 tsp. salt

pinch Chinese five-spice powder
3 whole chicken breasts, skinned,
    boned and cut into 1-inch cubes

BATTER

1/2 cup flour
1/4 cup cornstarch
1/4 tsp. baking powder

1/2 tsp. baking soda
1/4 tsp. rice vinegar
3/4 cup water

oil for deep frying

SAUCE

1 cup water
3/4 cup sugar
1/2 cup Rose's Lime Juice
1/4 tsp. salt
3 drops yellow food coloring

1 lemon with peel, thinly sliced, seeds
    removed
3 tbs. cornstarch
3 tbs. cold water

In a small bowl, combine water, sherry, garlic powder, salt and five-spice powder. Add chicken cubes and stir to coat well. Allow to stand for 30 minutes.

To prepare batter: In a small bowl, combine ingredients until smooth.

Heat oil in the deep fryer to 360°. Dip chicken cubes into batter and fry in batches until light golden and chicken is cooked through, about 2 to 3 minutes. Drain on paper towels. Place cooked chicken pieces in a low oven on a paper towel-lined cookie sheet. Repeat until all chicken is cooked through and sauce is prepared.

To prepare sauce: In a saucepan, combine water, sugar, lime juice, salt, food coloring and lemon. Bring to a boil over medium high heat. In a small bowl, combine cornstarch and cold water to make a smooth paste. Stir into mixture in saucepan and heat until clear, thick and bubbly.

Add chicken to sauce and serve hot.

SWEET AND SOUR CHINESE CHICKEN

Serve this delicious recipe over a bed of steamed rice; it's so colorful and flavorful!

SWEET AND SOUR SAUCE

¾ cup sugar
2 tbs. cornstarch
2 tbs. rice vinegar

3 tbs. ketchup
¾ cup water

BATTER

½ cup flour
¼ cup cornstarch
¼ tsp. baking powder
½ tsp. baking soda

¼ tsp. rice vinegar
¼ tsp. garlic powder
1 tsp. soy sauce
¾ cup water

oil for deep frying
2 whole chicken breasts, skinned, boned and cut into 1-inch cubes
steamed rice

GARNISHES

1 ripe red tomato, cut in wedges
1 green bell pepper, seeded and sliced

1 can (8 oz.) pineapple chunks, drained
1 tbs. toasted sesame seeds

Prepare sauce first. In a small saucepan, combine sugar and cornstarch. Add remaining ingredients and bring to a boil over medium high heat. Mixture should be thick and bubbly. Remove from heat and set aside.

To prepare batter: In a small bowl, whisk together ingredients until smooth.

Heat oil in the deep fryer to 360°. Dip chicken cubes into batter. Fry chicken cubes in batches until chicken is light golden and cooked through, about 2 to 3 minutes. Remove to paper towels to drain. Place cooked pieces in a low oven on a paper towel-lined cookie sheet. Repeat until all chicken is cooked through.

Place a mound of steamed rice on a large platter. Place chicken pieces on top and pour sauce over. Add garnishes.

CHICKEN MELON

The color and flavor contrasts in this recipe are beautiful and most unusual. Don't let all the steps and ingredients keep you from trying this delicious dish. Serve over a bed of steamed white rice and offer a light spinach salad to round out your menu.

3 tbs. soy sauce
3 tbs. sherry
2 whole chicken breasts, skinned, boned and cut into 1-inch cubes

BATTER

½ cup flour
¼ cup cornstarch
½ tsp. baking powder

½ tsp. baking soda
¼ tsp. rice vinegar
¾ cup water

SWEET AND SOUR SAUCE

3 tbs. cornstarch
3 tbs. brown sugar
3 tbs. cider vinegar

3 tbs. ketchup
1 tbs. soy sauce
1 cup pineapple juice

VEGETABLE AND FRUIT MIXTURE

2 tbs. peanut oil
1 green bell pepper, seeded and cut into 1-inch cubes
1 white onion, halved and cut into crescent slices

1 cucumber, peeled, seeded and cut diagonally into slices
1 small cantaloupe, peeled, seeded and cut into 1-inch cubes
½ cup whole skinned almonds

oil for deep frying

In a bowl, combine soy sauce and sherry and stir in chicken cubes. Allow to stand at room temperature to marinate while preparing remaining ingredients.

Combine batter ingredients until smooth. Pour into a bowl and set aside.

Combine sauce ingredients until smooth. Bring to a boil in a small saucepan and cook until thickened and bubbly. Keep warm.

Prepare vegetable and fruit mixture. Heat oil in a large skillet over medium high heat. Stir-fry green pepper and onion until tender-crisp. Add cucumber, cantaloupe and almonds. Stir to heat though.

Heat oil in the deep fryer to 360°. Dip chicken pieces into prepared batter. Fry chicken pieces in batches until light golden brown and cooked through. Remove and drain on paper towels. Keep warm in a low oven. When all chicken is cooked, place on a large platter, pour sauce over and top with vegetable and fruit mixture.

TEMPURA

*Here are some ideas for ideal tempura foods. Cut foods into even, bite-sized pieces. The secret to light and crispy tempura is having the batter icy cold and lumpy. A combination of cottonseed oil (¾) and light sesame oil (¼) gives a nice light oil for tempura. You can also use peanut oil. Serve with **Sesame Soy Dipping Sauce**, page 97; **Tartar Sauce**, page 114; or **Sweet and Sour Sauce**, page 134.*

asparagus tips
carrots, peeled and cut diagonally
   into ⅓-inch-thick slices
cauliflower
eggplant, peeled and cut into
   ½-inch-square fingers
ginger shoots
ginkgo nuts
green or red bell peppers, cut
   lengthwise into ½-inch-thick slices
Japanese radishes
lotus root, peeled and cut into
   ¼-inch-thick slices

mushrooms
onion rings
prawns or large shrimp
scallops
snow peas
string beans
sugar snap peas
sweet potatoes, peeled and cut into
   ⅓-inch-thick slices
white fish, cut into bite-sized pieces
zucchini, cut diagonally into
   ⅓-inch-thick slices

BATTER

1 cup ice cold water
1 egg
¼ tsp. baking soda
¼ tsp. salt

¼ tsp. soy sauce
1 cup unsifted cake flour
⅓ cup unsifted cake flour

oil for deep frying

Prepare tempura foods.

To prepare batter: Combine water, egg, soda, salt, soy sauce and 1 cup cake flour until batter is very smooth. Pour into a bowl and set it in a larger bowl filled half full with ice cubes and water. Sprinkle ⅓ cup cake flour over top of batter and stir lightly with a fork; batter should still be very lumpy.

Heat oil in the deep fryer to 375°. Dip prepared foods into batter and allow excess batter to drip back into bowl. Fry several pieces at once, but do not overcrowd fryer. Food should be tender-crisp in 2 to 3 minutes. Serve immediately with dipping sauces.

CHICKEN INDIA

This style of marinating chicken in yogurt and spices comes from India. Serve with rice pilaf, chutney and cucumber salad.

1 whole chicken, about 2½-3 lb.
2 cups plain yogurt
½ cup lemon juice
½ tsp. ground coriander
½ tsp. chili powder
½ tsp. ground turmeric
½ tsp. ground cumin
2 cloves garlic, minced
1½ cups flour
1 tsp. curry powder
1 tsp. salt
½ tsp. pepper
oil for deep frying

Rinse chicken and pat dry with paper towels. Quarter chicken by cutting lengthwise down the backbone with poultry shears or a sharp knife. Remove backbone and wing tips. In a large bowl, combine yogurt, lemon juice, coriander, chili powder, turmeric, cumin and garlic. Add chicken pieces and turn to coat well. Cover and refrigerate overnight. In a large plastic bag, combine flour, curry powder, salt and pepper. Remove chicken from marinade and place in plastic bag. Shake well to coat with flour. Heat oil in the deep fryer to 350°. Add leg pieces first and fry for 5 minutes. Add breast pieces and continue cooking for 15 minutes or until cooked through. Drain on paper towels.

SIDE DISHES

ONION RINGS

This recipe is unique due to the method of soaking the onion rings in ice water to make them extra crisp and mild. For more spicy onion rings, add a bit of cayenne.

1½ lb. large Spanish onions, about 2
1½ cups flour
2 tbs. cornmeal
2 tsp. baking powder
1½ tsp. salt
¼ tsp. pepper

dash cayenne pepper, optional
1¼ cups milk
2 eggs, separated
1 tbs. vegetable oil
oil for deep frying

Peel onions and cut into ½-inch-thick slices. Separate into rings and place in a large bowl; cover with ice water. Chill for 30 minutes. In a large bowl, combine flour, cornmeal, baking powder, salt and peppers. In another bowl, combine milk, egg yolks and vegetable oil; beat well. Add to dry ingredients and stir well to combine. In a third bowl, beat egg whites until stiff peaks form. Fold egg whites into batter. Drain chilled onion rings on paper towel. Heat oil in the deep fryer to 375°. Dip onion rings into batter and fry in batches for 3 to 5 minutes or until golden brown. Drain on paper towels.

ONION RING LOAF

Servings: 4-8

One of our favorite restaurant chains is Tony Roma's. They serve a delicious onion ring loaf that is a lot of fun to eat. You can prepare this at home using the basket of your deep fryer. Serve with ketchup and barbecue sauce for dipping. Depending on the size and shape of your basket, this recipe will serve 4 to 8.

2 lb. large yellow onions
1 cup milk
1 egg
2 tsp. sugar

¼ cup flour, or more as needed
oil for deep frying
salt

Peel onions and slice into ⅜-inch-thick slices. Pop out into rings; reserve centers for another use, if desired, and use only large outer rings, of at least 1½-inch diameter. In a large bowl, combine milk, egg, sugar and ¼ cup flour. Add onion rings and mix it all together with your hands until rings are lightly coated and no longer sticky. Add more flour as needed. Refrigerate rings in batter for at least 2 hours before cooking. Heat oil in the deep fryer to 360°. Fill fryer basket with rings; pile them in loosely — do not press them down. Slide basket into hot oil; press top of rings down with a slotted spoon to completely submerge in hot oil. Cook for 3 minutes or until golden and crispy. Shake off excess oil, and sprinkle with salt.

CORN AND JALAPEÑO FRITTERS

Servings: 8

For variety, add a scant cup of either drained canned clams or chopped ham.

1 cup corn kernels, fresh, frozen or
   canned
3 eggs, beaten
½ cup crushed soda cracker crumbs
½ tsp. salt

½ tsp. pepper
1 jalapeño pepper, seeded and
   finely chopped
oil for deep frying
Sour Cream and Salsa Dip, follows

Place corn in a medium bowl. Stir in eggs, crumbs, salt, pepper and jalapeño. Heat oil in the deep fryer to 375°. Using a spoon, scoop batter into hot oil, using another spoon to slide batter off. Fry fritters in batches until golden, about 4 minutes. Drain on paper towels. Serve with *Sour Cream and Salsa Dip*.

SOUR CREAM AND SALSA DIP

1 cup sour cream
⅔ cup prepared tomato salsa

In a small bowl, combine ingredients. Refrigerate any leftover dip. Makes 1⅔ cups.

FRENCH FRIES

Although a simple food, making good French fries requires several steps. Read the directions carefully to master the technique. Leaving the peels on the potatoes gives a more rustic appearance and retains more vitamins.

2 lb. baking potatoes   salt
oil for deep frying

Peel potatoes, if desired. Cut potatoes lengthwise into ⅜-inch slices and again into ⅜-inch strips. Soak in cold water for 30 minutes, changing water once. Rinse well in cold water to remove surface starch and blot dry with paper towels. Heat oil in the deep fryer to 325°. If you are using the fryer basket, heat it in oil as well. Drop potatoes into hot oil in batches, stirring to prevent them from sticking. (If using the basket, be sure to lower it very slowly to prevent oil from splattering and bubbling.) Cook potatoes for about 3 minutes or until cooked through but not brown. The potatoes will really bubble up due to all the moisture released when frying. Drain cooked fries on paper towels; fry remaining batches.

Reheat the same oil to 375°. Cook fries again for 3 to 5 minutes or until potatoes have almost stopped bubbling. Repeat with remaining batches. Drain fries on paper towels and sprinkle with salt. Keep warm in a low oven on a paper towel-lined cookie sheet.

VARIATION: POTATO CHIPS

To make your own potato chips, use a very thin potato slice. A food processor is a great help in making the slices consistently thin. Pat the slices dry with a paper towel. Make sure oil is sufficiently preheated to 325°. Do not overcrowd your fryer. A frying basket will simplify placing chips in fryer. If you don't have one, use a slotted spoon. It is important to lower chips slowly into hot oil. While potatoes are cooking, with a slotted spoon separate any pieces that are sticking together. The chips will bubble furiously as the moisture cooks away. When the bubbling stops, chips are done. Drain on paper towels and sprinkle with salt.

SQUASH PUPPIES

Servings: 8

A great way to sneak vegetables to your kids! Mixture can be made up to 3 days ahead, refrigerated and fried at your convenience.

4 medium yellow summer squash
salted water
1 onion, finely chopped
1 cup shredded sharp cheddar cheese
½ cup cornmeal
1 tsp. baking powder
1 tsp. salt
½ tsp. pepper
1 egg, beaten
oil for deep frying

Cut squash in quarters. Place in a large pan and cover with salted water. Bring to a boil over medium high heat and cook until squash is very tender, about 10 minutes. Drain well and mash. Add remaining ingredients and mix well. Cover and store in the refrigerator until needed. To fry, heat oil in the deep fryer to 375°. Drop by spoonfuls into hot oil. Cook until golden brown, about 3 to 4 minutes. Remove and drain on paper towels. Serve hot.

VEGETABLES

ALMOND-CRUSTED
SWEET POTATO BALLS

Here's something different for the holidays. These go well with chicken, pork or turkey. Adding a pinch of salt to the egg whites breaks up the viscosity. You can use canned sweet potatoes in this recipe, but be sure to drain them well.

4 large sweet potatoes	1 tsp. salt
2 eggs, separated	pinch salt
1/4 cup sweet sherry	1 1/2 cups blanched almonds
1/4 tsp. freshly grated nutmeg	oil for deep frying

Boil sweet potatoes until tender. Cool, peel and mash thoroughly. You should have about 3 cups. Stir in egg yolks, sherry, nutmeg and 1 tsp. salt; mix well. In a shallow dish, whisk egg whites with pinch salt. Chop almonds coarsely and place in another shallow dish. Form sweet potatoes into 1-inch balls. Dip into egg whites, and roll in almonds. Place on a cookie sheet, cover with plastic wrap and refrigerate for 1 hour or up to 24 hours. To fry, heat oil in the deep fryer to 375°. Fry balls in batches until almonds are golden and balls are cooked through, about 3 to 4 minutes. Drain on paper towels. Serve hot.

SWEET POTATO FRITTERS

Serve these unusual fritters for a special brunch. Be sure to have plenty of hot maple syrup to drizzle on top. You can add ½ cup crisp, crumbled bacon or finely chopped ham to the batter for a change of pace. Shred the sweet potatoes by hand or with the shredding disc of a food processor.

2 cups flour
2 tsp. baking powder
1 tsp. salt
1⅓ cup milk
4 eggs, beaten
¼ cup butter, melted

4 cups coarsely shredded sweet
  potatoes
½ cup cooked crumbled bacon
oil for deep frying
¼ cup powdered sugar
maple syrup

In a large bowl, combine flour, baking powder and salt. Add milk, eggs and melted butter. Mix well. Stir in sweet potatoes and bacon. Heat oil in the deep fryer to 370°. Drop batter by spoonfuls into hot oil. Fry in batches until crispy and golden, about 4 minutes. Drain well on paper towels. Sprinkle with powdered sugar and serve hot with maple syrup.

CRISPY ONION RINGS

Serve these delicious morsels piled high and lightly sprinkled with salt. They can be made ahead and stored in the refrigerator for up to 3 days, which makes them ideal for entertaining. Reheat them on a cookie sheet in a 350° oven for 3 minutes.

1 lb. onions, peeled and thinly sliced
½ cup flour
½ tsp. paprika
½ tsp. white pepper
½ tsp. garlic powder
oil for deep frying

Separate onions into rings. In a paper bag, combine flour and seasonings. Shake onions in bag to coat evenly with flour. Heat oil in the deep fryer to 300°. Fry onions in batches until crisp and golden, about 5 minutes. Drain on paper towels. Keep warm in a low oven.

CARROT AND PARSNIP FRITTERS

Servings: 6-8

If you are not familiar with parsnips, we urge you to try this recipe. They are delightfully sweet.

1 cup parsnips
1 cup carrots
½ cup onion
2 eggs, beaten
½-1 cup flour
1 tsp. salt
½ tsp. pepper
1 tbs. chopped fresh parsley
oil for deep frying

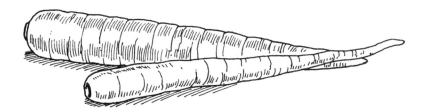

Shred vegetables by hand or with the shredding disc of a food processor. In a large bowl, combine vegetables, eggs, ½ cup flour and seasonings. Add more flour if needed to make fritters hold their shape. Heat oil in the deep fryer to 390°. Drop batter by spoonfuls into hot oil and fry until golden brown. Drain on paper towels. Serve hot.

ZUCCHINI FRITTERS

Serve with ranch dressing as a dipping sauce.

2 cups shredded zucchini, with peel
½ cup shredded onion
2 eggs, beaten
½ cup grated Parmesan cheese
½-1 cup flour
½ tsp. pepper
1 tbs. chopped fresh parsley
oil for deep frying

In a large bowl, combine zucchini, onion, eggs, cheese and enough flour to make fritters hold their shape. Start with ½ cup and then add more if needed after frying the first one. Stir in pepper and parsley. Heat oil in the deep fryer to 390°. Drop batter by spoonfuls and fry until golden brown. Drain on paper towels.

TRI-COLORED PEPPER RINGS

Keep these warm in a 200° oven while frying remainder.

¾ cup fine dry breadcrumbs
2 tbs. grated Parmesan cheese
1 tsp. onion salt
¼ tsp. garlic powder
2 egg whites, beaten
2 tbs. water

1 red bell pepper, cut in ½-inch rings
1 green bell pepper, cut in ½-inch rings
1 yellow bell pepper, cut in ½-inch rings
oil for deep frying
Curry Dip, follows

Combine breadcrumbs, cheese, onion salt and garlic powder; set aside. Whisk together egg whites and water. Dip pepper rings into egg white mixture; coat with breadcrumb mixture. Heat oil in the deep fryer to 350°. Fry rings in batches until golden brown and crispy, about 2 to 3 minutes. Drain on paper towels. Serve with *Curry Dip*.

CURRY DIP

1 cup mayonnaise
2 tbs. bottled chili sauce
1 tsp. minced onion

1 tsp. tarragon vinegar
1 tsp. curry powder

Combine ingredients. Cover and chill. Makes 1 cup.

DESSERTS

DESSERT RAVIOLI WITH RASPBERRY SAUCE AND CHOCOLATE

Frequently you can find large, round ravioli filled with ricotta, which are ideal for this recipe. They make a stunning presentation when served on a white or clear glass dessert plate. Garnish with a mint leaf or small flower.

1 lb. cheese-filled ravioli
oil for deep frying
Raspberry Sauce, page 165

1 bar (4 oz.) semisweet chocolate,
  shaved
1/4 cup powdered sugar

Cook ravioli as directed on package. Drain well. Spread on paper towels in a single layer and use another paper towel to blot excess moisture. Heat oil in the deep fryer to 370°. Fry cooked ravioli in batches until golden brown, about 5 minutes. Drain on paper towels. Swirl *Raspberry Sauce* on individual dessert plates. Place 3 to 4 ravioli on each plate. Top with shaved chocolate and sprinkle with powdered sugar.

NOTE: To shave chocolate, simply run a potato peeler down the edge of a bar of chocolate, or use a grater.

ROSETTES

For this recipe, you will need a rosette iron, which you can easily find at department stores and kitchen stores. Follow the instructions carefully and you will get great results on these rather temperamental delicacies.

HINTS FOR MAKING PERFECT ROSETTES

1. Only make *Rosettes* on a clear, dry day; a humid day will spoil the results.
2. Use a good rosette iron made of cast aluminum; light weight irons do not work well.
3. Invite a friend over to help, and make an assembly line to prepare *Rosettes*. To make an efficient working pattern, have one person form *Rosettes* and the other cook and drain.
4. Have plenty of cookie sheets on hand.
5. Be sure to have plenty of locking freezer bags on hand.
6. *Rosettes* freeze well and do not require thawing.
7. Handle *Rosettes* gently.
8. After preparing batter, allow it to "rest" in the refrigerator for 30 minutes to allow the gluten in the flour to relax.
9. It is important to keep the oil temperature at 400° at all times.
10. Keep the rosette iron in the hot oil at all times.
11. Do not count on the first couple of *Rosettes* turning out well — those are for the cook to sample. Residual oil from the iron will combine with the batter making later versions better.
12. Make at least two batches of batter at a time, since you are going to all this work anyway, but do not double the batches.

2 eggs
1 cup whole milk
½ tsp. salt
2 tsp. sugar

1 cup sifted flour
oil for deep frying
powdered sugar

Place eggs, milk, salt, sugar and flour in a food processor or blender. Mix well. Pour batter through a fine wire mesh sieve into a shallow pie pan. Refrigerate for 30 minutes. Batter should be the consistency of heavy cream. To prepare *Rosettes*, heat oil in the deep fryer to 400°. Remove batter from the refrigerator; whisk well with a fork. Heat rosette iron in oil until very hot; shake off excess oil. Gently dip iron into batter no more than ¾ of the way up the side. Immediately submerge iron in hot oil. Fry for a few seconds; shake iron in oil to release *Rosette*. Allow *Rosette* to float free to brown lightly; gently turn over with a long-handled, two-pronged fork. When light golden brown on both sides, gently remove from oil and drain on paper towels. Make a single layer only; do not stack. When all *Rosettes* are made and cooled, stack 5 at a time in a bowl and sift powdered sugar over them. Place into locking freezer bags if you are going to freeze them. Just before serving, dust again with powdered sugar, if desired.

DUTCH APPLE FRITTERS

Raisins and a hint of lemon add flavor to this old Dutch recipe.

1 cup sugar
3 cups flour
4 tsp. baking powder
1 tsp. freshly grated nutmeg
1/2 tsp. salt
2 eggs, beaten
1 cup milk

1 1/2 tsp. lemon extract
1 cup raisins
1/2 cup flour
2 apples, peeled and finely chopped
1 cup sugar
2 tsp. cinnamon
oil for deep frying

In a large bowl, combine sugar, flour, baking powder, nutmeg and salt. Add eggs, milk and lemon extract; stir well. In a small bowl, combine raisins and flour; coat raisins well. Add raisins to batter and stir in apples. In a locking freezer bag, combine sugar and cinnamon; set aside. Heat oil in the deep fryer to 370°. Drop batter by teaspoonfuls into fryer. Fry in batches until crispy and golden, about 4 minutes. Drain on paper towels. While still hot, shake in cinnamon sugar. Serve warm.

QUICK SOPAIPILLAS WITH CINNAMON HONEY SAUCE

This makes a great dessert after a Mexican meal. Sopaipillas are usually made out of a yeast dough, but this easy variation uses flour tortillas. It's fun to serve these on a big platter in the center of the table. You might offer different flavors of ice cream toppings to go alongside. Guests can help themselves to crispy, sweet tortillas; smooth, cold ice cream; and strawberry or chocolate sundae topping. Give each person a dessert plate and plenty of napkins.

1 pkg. (12 oz.) flour tortillas
oil for deep frying
1 cup honey

1 tbs. cinnamon
½ gal. vanilla ice cream

Cut tortillas into wedges. Heat oil in the deep fryer to 375°. Fry tortilla wedges in batches until puffy and golden. Remove and drain on paper towels. Keep warm in a low oven on a cookie sheet while frying remainder. In a saucepan over medium heat, melt honey with cinnamon. To serve, mound tortillas on a large platter. Drizzle with honey and top with scoops of ice cream.

FRIED PEACHES WITH VANILLA SAUCE

Be sure to blot the fruit very dry with paper towels to avoid spatters.

2 cups flour
½ tsp. salt
1 tsp. sugar
1 can (12 oz.) beer
4 egg whites, beaten until stiff
¼ cup sugar

1 tsp. cinnamon
oil for deep frying
4 fresh peaches, peeled, pitted and
  quartered
Vanilla Sauce, follows

In a bowl, combine flour, salt and 1 tsp. sugar. Slowly stir in beer until batter is smooth and creamy; fold in egg whites. Combine sugar and cinnamon; set aside. Heat oil in the deep fryer to 370°. Dip fruit in batter; fry until light golden brown, about 2 minutes. Drain on paper towels; sprinkle with cinnamon sugar. Serve with *Vanilla Sauce*.

VANILLA SAUCE

1 pt. half-and-half
¼ cup sugar

2 tsp. vanilla extract
5 egg yolks

In the top of a double boiler, combine cream, sugar and vanilla. Bring to a boil. In a bowl, whisk egg yolks. Add a bit of boiling cream to eggs, stirring well. Turn heat to low and add egg mixture to cream; cook until thickened, stirring constantly.

CANDIED PECANS

These addictive nibbles make a wonderful gift at holiday time. Store these in an airtight container. Freeze if keeping longer than 48 hours.

¾ cup water
3 tbs. sugar
2 tbs. honey

2 cups pecan halves
oil for deep frying

In a saucepan, combine water, sugar and honey. Bring to a boil and boil for 1 minute. Reduce heat to medium and add nuts. Cook for 15 minutes, stirring occasionally, until most of the liquid has simmered away. Heat oil in the deep fryer to 275°. Add nuts and fry, stirring often, until deep brown, about 8 minutes. Drain on paper towels, separating nuts so that they do not stick together. Cool until glaze is hard.

IDEAS FOR FRIED ICE CREAM

Fried ice cream is such a festive dessert to make and eat! Here are some ideas for combinations to try. Kids love this dessert and, when entertaining a small group of guests, it's a real conversation piece. Be sure to use your prettiest dessert plates and be creative with garnishes. A bit of whipped cream, an orange slice, a scatter of berries, a slice of starfruit or kiwi, a few shavings of dark chocolate, some chopped nuts or a sprinkle of cocoa — all add visual interest to the plate. Try adding a fresh flower; pansies make a delightful garnish.

- rum raisin ice cream with raisin bread and butterscotch sauce
- peach ice cream with blueberry sauce
- strawberry ice cream with strawberry sauce
- macadamia nut ice cream with pineapple sauce
- coffee ice cream with fudge sauce
- peppermint ice cream with fudge sauce
- chocolate ice cream with fudge sauce
- butter brickle ice cream with toffee sauce
- pralines and cream ice cream with caramel sauce
- for adults only: try adding a bit of liqueur or brandy to your sauce

MEXICAN FRIED ICE CREAM

This popular dessert is served in Mexican restaurants. The secret to having it turn out well is to prepare the ice cream balls several days ahead and place them in the coldest part of your freezer. Have your deep fryer ready to go and take the ice cream balls directly from the freezer and place in the fryer. Watch very carefully and remove ice cream as soon as it looks crispy. Serve immediately. Time is of the essence on this one. Serve with sliced fresh strawberries and whipped cream.

½ gal. French vanilla ice cream
3 cups crushed Frosted Flakes cereal
4 tsp. cinnamon
oil for deep frying

Shape ice cream into 8 balls. In a shallow bowl, combine Frosted Flakes and cinnamon. Roll each ice cream ball in cereal. Place on a cookie sheet and freeze until very hard. To fry, heat oil in the deep fryer to 375°. Remove ice cream balls from freezer, one at a time, and fry briefly until golden, about 5 seconds. Serve immediately.

FRIED ICE CREAM WITH RASPBERRY SAUCE

Make as many servings of this delightful dessert as you desire.

1 ball vanilla ice cream or flavor of
  your choice
2 slices soft white bread, crusts removed
oil for deep frying
Raspberry Sauce, follows
whipped cream, optional
fresh fruit, optional

    Working quickly, mold slices of bread firmly around ice cream ball to enclose completely. Wrap tightly in plastic wrap to hold bread snug around ice cream. Freeze.

    When ready to serve, heat oil in the deep fryer to 375°. Take ice cream ball directly from freezer, unwrap and fry until golden. Serve immediately with *Raspberry Sauce* and garnish with whipped cream and fresh fruit, if desired.

RASPBERRY SAUCE

1 pkg. (10 oz.) frozen raspberries, thawed
1 tbs. cornstarch
1 tbs. sugar
1 tbs. lemon juice

Puree raspberries in a food processor or blender. Press through a sieve to remove seeds. Combine cornstarch, sugar and lemon juice. Add to raspberries and bring to a boil in a small saucepan, stirring until thickened. Chill before serving. Makes 1½ cups.

DATE AND GINGER WON TONS

A wonderful dessert for an Oriental meal. The bright-colored yellow skin of the lemon is the rind or zest; do not use the pulpy white membrane underneath, which is bitter.

1 cup chopped dates
2 tbs. finely chopped crystallized ginger
½ cup chopped macadamia nuts
juice of ½ lemon

2 tsp. grated lemon zest
40 won ton wrappers
oil for deep frying
powdered sugar

Using a food processor or blender, combine dates, ginger, nuts, lemon juice and zest. Place 1 tsp. date mixture in the center of each won ton wrapper. Fold edge over filling and roll to within 1 inch of the corner. Moisten edges of won ton wrapper with water and fold corners over, overlapping the points slightly. Pinch together to seal. (See diagram on page 27.) Place filled won tons on a cookie sheet in a single layer. At this point, these may be covered with plastic wrap and refrigerated for up to 24 hours. To fry, heat oil in the deep fryer to 350°. Fry won tons in batches until crisp and golden, about 2 minutes. Drain on paper towels. Sprinkle generously with powdered sugar. Filling retains heat, so cool before serving.

INDEX